THE LAST
FRONTIER
THE ROMAN INVASIONS OF SCOTLAND

For Eileen,
who is Scottish,
another Roman book

THE LAST
FRONTIER

THE ROMAN INVASIONS OF SCOTLAND

TEMPUS

First published 2004

Tempus Publishing Limited
The Mill, Brimscombe Port,
Stroud, Gloucestershire, GL5 2QG
www.tempus-publishing.com

© Antony Kamm, 2004

Outline maps by Jennifer Campbell

The right of Antony Kamm to be identified as the Author
of this work has been asserted in accordance with the
Copyrights, Designs and Patents Act 1988.

British Library Cataloguing in Publication Data.
A catalogue record for this book is available from the British Library.

ISBN 0 7524 3137 4

Typesetting and origination by Tempus Publishing Limited
Printed and bound in Great Britain

CONTENTS

PREFACE

In attempting to put the Roman involvement with Scotland into its historical context and in a narrative and chronological form, I have referred to the sources listed at the end of this book. I take full responsibility, however, for any conclusions drawn from the evidence, and for unattributed translations from classical texts.

Almost all the places, geographical features, and peoples mentioned in the text are included in one or more of the maps, as indicated in the index. An individual's dates, as far as they are known, are usually cited on the first occasion he or she appears in the text, and also in the index.

My special thanks are due to Geoff Bailey, Bob Cowan, Ian Keillar, Lawrence Keppie, and Alan Senior for help with sources, to Ian Keillar, too, for information, to Jacqueline Kuijpers for resolving a point of Latin, to David Levinson for thoughts on Tacitus, and to Stirling University Library for loans, inter-library loan facilities, and document delivery services. I am grateful also to former and present members of the staff of Tempus: to Peter Kemmis Betty for advice, to Tim Clarke, who commissioned this book, to Emma Parkin, who saw it through its early stages, to Fran Gannon, who took over from her and also put the place names on the maps, and to Alex Cameron and freelance proof reader Margaret Haynes for their comments.

Antony Kamm
Dollar, Clackmannanshire
September 2004

LIST OF MAPS

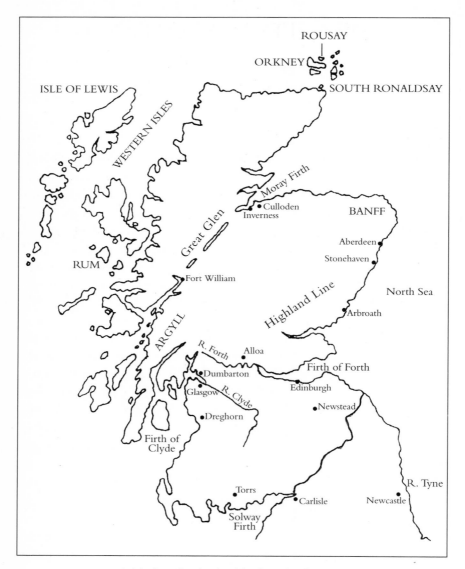

1 Modern Scotland, with places in chapter 1

1

THE CELTS IN SCOTLAND

Britain was still attached to the European mainland by a series of undulating valleys, when, about 18,000 years ago, the ice that covered most of Scotland began to recede. Glacial erosion carved the landscape into mountainous cliffs and corries, plateaux crossed by gullies and chasms, and, in lowland areas, rocky hills and lochs. Britain became finally separated from the mainland in about 6000 BC. By then there had been people in Scotland for some time. Almost certainly they arrived well before the date of the earliest known settlement, at Kinloch, on the island of Rum, which has been put at 7600 BC.

In the milder climate that followed the disappearance of the ice, trees, migrating from southern Britain and from the continent, replaced the shrubs, grass, and ferns which covered much of the landscape. The first of these was birch, around 7800 BC, followed by hazel. Northernmost Scotland and the islands around, however, retained their character of open scrub woodland for another 4,000 years. By about 5000 BC, pine and birch dominated the rest of the north-west, with oak and hazel to the north-east. Oak, elm, and hazel grew widely in central and lowland areas. The spreading woodlands, varying in their density according to the location, and the resources of the sea and of the lakes and rivers offered abundant opportunities for groups of hunter-gatherers, whose predecessors had followed the reindeer as the herds moved northward.

The new inhabitants were coastal people, skilled navigators of the lochs and inlets, and even of the sea itself, in dug-out canoes and skin-covered craft. They made a wide range of tools for their needs: axe-heads, scrapers, cutters, and pointed instruments from flint, hammer-heads from stone, and fish-hooks and barbed heads for arrows and harpoons from bone and antler. They lived in caves or wood-framed huts; tents of dressed skins provided shelter on hunting expeditions.

A varied diet was amply available, especially to island or coastal communities. Refuse tips of the time have revealed discarded shells of more than 20 species of shellfish, as well as the bones of cod, haddock, turbot, coalfish, bream, and dog-fish, some of which could only have been caught with a line from a boat. The remains of over 30 kinds of bird have been identified, including the extinct great auk. Meat was red deer, roe deer, wild boar, and smaller animals and marine mammals, while coastal pastures provided grass and seaweed, and the forests nuts and acorns.

There is evidence of woodland management and agricultural activity, on the part either of the hunter-gatherers or of new immigrants, from about 5000 BC, when the climate became more favourable and thus sea voyages safer. Farming brought not only a radical change in lifestyle, with settled communities and new food resources, but also new economic practices and technologies. Elm trees tend to favour the better soils, and these were the first to be cleared with stone or flint axes for agricultural land; the process was assisted by an outbreak of Dutch elm disease in about 3800 BC.

The new settlers grew cereal crops, mainly wheat and barley, and kept cattle, goats, pigs, and sheep, as well as dogs. They lived for the most part in permanent settlements of timber-framed houses with turf or earth walls, from which they moved to summer grazings or fishing grounds. On the Argyll coast are several sites dating to about 4000 BC which may have been processing plants for fish and shellfish. The people of the time made earthenware pots for cooking and storage. Their dead were buried in earth barrows, chambered cairns, or underground tombs constructed of stone. From one of these, a cairn with several compartments and three cells opening off the main chamber, at Isbister, South Ronaldsay, the remains have been recovered of some 340 men, women, and children, interred from about 3200 to 2800 BC. The average height of the men was about 5ft 7in (1.70m) and of the women 5ft 4in (1.63m), much the same as today. Life expectancy, however, was comparatively short; of the few who reached their fifties, most were men. Spine injuries and broken bones were commonplace, testifying to lives of heavy labour. Many of the skulls of the women were damaged by carrying loads by means of a band across the forehead.

The most astonishing traces of the early British farming culture are in the most unsuitable landscape, the northern isles of Scotland. At some point agricultural settlers sailed to Orkney and Shetland, and outlying islands, bringing with them their flocks. The bird-cherry, wild-cherry, and sloe grew there then, but otherwise the land was virtually treeless, and dominated by shrub and bare heath. In this inhospitable terrain, something more substantial than a shack was required to keep out the blasting wind and howling gales. On the coast of the tiny Orkney island of Papa Westray the remains have been found of two adjoining houses with access from one to the other, occupied between about 3600 and 3100 BC. They are built from local flagstones, laid flat, with refuse packed into the walls as insulation. One has two rooms; the second may have been utilised as a storehouse or workroom, and is lined with cupboards.

The complex of stone dwellings at Skara Brae, Orkney, was occupied between about 3100 and 2450 BC, that is some 1,500 years before the destruction of Troy by the Greeks. Part of a settlement, it comprises several single-room apartments with walls 6ft 6in (2m) thick. These were linked by underground passageways and equipped with a peat-burning hearth, a box-bed, shelves or cupboards, and a serviceable dresser. Slab-lined boxes inset into the stone flooring were probably for keeping fresh shellfish. There is evidence of an internal drainage system, which in the case of a similar site at Rinyo on the island of Rousay was lined with hazel bark. It has recently been suggested that a house at Skara Brae set slightly apart from the others may have incorporated brewing facilities; if so, it is the earliest-known alehouse in Britain.

These homes were semi-subterranean, and probably roofed with turfs on driftwood or whalebone supports. Layers of rubbish were dumped on top. From these, and from the buildings themselves, has been recovered a range of artefacts and other remains, including organic material, from which it has proved possible to reconstruct something of the lifestyle of the inhabitants of Skara Brae. While it may not be typical of that in other parts of Scotland, the finds illustrate the ingenuity and resourcefulness of the age.

It has been suggested that the traces of yellow iris indicate some medicinal use, possibly to ease bowel problems caused by a diet lacking in plant fibre. The mature puffballs recovered may have been to staunch bleeding, which would have been a common hazard when sharp stone knives or flints were used in semi-darkness and on slippery floors to scrape skins, cut meat, or shape artefacts. Puffballs were still utilised for this purpose by surgeons and in farmhouses in the nineteenth century. Tools and other implements were fashioned from animal and whale bones, and pins, including some as long as 9½in (24cm), perhaps for skewering hair in place, from walrus ivory. Cooking utensils such as spatulae and stirring rods were made of wood. Flat-bottomed pots and bowls, known as grooved ware, were decorated with grooves, incisions, or strips of clay. The desire for decoration extended to ceremonial objects such as polished stone mace heads, and intricately carved stone balls, 2½in (7cm) in diameter, of which some 400 examples have been found in Scotland.

Grooved ware occurs in many parts of Britain, but examples found in Scotland are earlier than those in England. Pottery of this kind unearthed at Dreghorn, Ayrshire, in 2004 has enabled the site, which dates from about 3500 BC, to be tentatively identified as Britain's oldest continually-inhabited village.

In about 2900 BC the elaborate chambered cairns and tombs gave way to the construction of more mysterious centres of ritual. A henge is an arrangement of monumental standing stones and timber, surrounded by a ditch with a bank outside it, as though the purpose was to enclose something inside, rather than keep things out, as would be the case with a defensive ditch. The monument could take other forms, as it does in the case of the Callanish stones on the Isle of Lewis. Here, a shaped megalith 15ft 6in (4.75m) high, is encircled by 13 standing stones. The approach from the north is by a double line of stones 80m long, with shorter single lines branching off to the east, south, and west, giving the effect of a huge cross. Within the centre circle is a small chambered tomb. Henges and other arrangements of standing stones such as Callanish were places of worship. By lining up the stones and timbers with the sun, moon, planets, and stars, a relationship could be suggested between heavenly powers and human presences.

The first metal-workers in Scotland were descendants of the original farmers, to whom the techniques were first introduced in about 2000 BC by craftsmen from the European mainland and from Ireland. Copper and gold could be dug from the ground, especially in south-west Scotland. Yet the most significant concentration of objects and stone moulds that has been discovered is north-east of a line which could be drawn between Inverness and Aberdeen. The settlers had become traders as well as farmers and craftsmen. Bronze, the next development, is an alloy of copper and tin, the only source of which in Britain is Cornwall, involving a journey from the north-east mainly by water, along the Great Glen (Inverness to Fort William) and then by sea. Disc-wheels of ash wood, for carts, unearthed in the Forth valley and dating from about 1000 BC, represent the earliest evidence for wheeled transport in Britain and Ireland. Pack animals would also have been employed.

Flat and flanged axe-heads, halberds, armlets, daggers, rapiers, spear-heads, bracelets, and razors are among the bronze objects that have been found. Gold was fashioned into jewellery, to make discs, earrings, and crescent-shaped collars. Elaborate necklaces were made of jet beads, the finest of which were imported to Scotland from east Yorkshire.

In general, however, the people of this period worked at subsistence farming on land demarcated by field walls. They tilled their land with simple ox-drawn wooden ploughs (known as ards), sometimes tipped with stone. The main crop was barley, with also some emmer wheat. Cattle, goats, sheep, and pigs were reared. The remains have been dis-covered of roundhouses of timber and stone, with thatched roofs, some 23ft (7m) in diameter. The undefended hut circles of the second mil-lennium BC had, by about 600 BC, given way to stockaded homes and settlements, and stone-walled hill-forts laced with timber. Massive cul-tural and economic changes were taking place in times that were often violent, of which the deliberate burying of locally produced bronze objects provides further evidence. These changes are associated with a society known generically as the Celts, who, according to classical sources, go back to 500 BC. Their origins, however, have been placed some 700 years earlier, at least.

The term 'Celtic' has come to describe a language, objects connect-ed with the Iron-Age tribes of central and north-western Europe, or ethnic or racial groups of people speaking a Celtic language or belong-ing to such a society. The Irish and Scottish Gaelic languages, and also Manx, are known as Q-Celtic, as distinct from P-Celtic (in which the 'qu' and 'k' sounds become a 'p' sound), such as Welsh, Cornish, and Breton. It is possible that an earlier version of both was one of the com-mon languages which had been employed for the purposes of trade since about 2000 BC. Certainly there appears to have been a close rela-tionship between the vernacular spoken in Britain and in Gaul. It is from this Gallo-Brittonnic dialect that the language of the Picts of Scotland is believed to have developed.

The Celts of the European mainland had acquired from immigrants from the Middle East a knowledge of agriculture, and crafts such as pottery and the construction of tools, as well as building. Their use of iron enabled them more easily to cut down forests as building materials and to open up land for farming. Their standard weapon, the iron slashing sword, revolutionised warfare for a time.

Unlike the Egyptians, Israelites, Greeks, and Romans, however, Celts did not use the art of writing to any great extent until about AD 450, relying on oral tradition and communication. Thus they were cut off from the accumulated wisdom and history of other civilisations, and our knowledge of them from literature of the times comes entirely from classical sources. The Romans referred to them as 'barbarians' simply because to them anyone was a barbarian who lived outside the frontiers of the Roman empire. And by 1000 BC societies of these Celtic-speaking barbarians were widely dispersed throughout Britain and Ireland. As well as their language, they brought their customs, their religion, their stories, their songs, their skills (including road building), their horses, and their taste for battle. Pedestrian paths were constructed of brushwood, planks, or hurdles set longitudinally. Roads used by wagons were made of timbers laid transversely and raised on causeways where the ground was heavy or waterlogged. The Celtic economy was based on agriculture; their warriors defended their lands against encroachers (usually other Celtic tribes); their skilled artists and craftsmen produced quality goods for the aristocracy and for export, in return for wine and luxury items. Celtic coins began to be produced in Britain at the end of the second century BC, but the tribes in Scotland did not use money, relying instead on barter.

The Romans subsisted on a balanced diet including wholewheat, vegetables, and fish, whereas the Celts were primarily meat-eaters, especially of pork, roast or boiled in a cauldron. (According to the Roman historian Cassius Dio (c.AD 160–c.235), who wrote in Greek, the Celts in central and northern Scotland ate no fish at all, in spite of the quantities available.) Ceremonial feasts were held round an open hearth in a roundhouse or out of doors, participants being seated in order of importance. Behind each warrior stood his armour-bearer. Hunks of meat were lifted up in the hands and gnawed. For a king in Ireland it was a leg of pork, for a queen a haunch. The 'champion's portion' went to the man regarded as the bravest, which often led to fighting on the spot.

The Celts were said to eat and drink hugely, but to have good table manners. The native drinks were mead or beer, though the Gauls in particular drank enormous quantities of undiluted Italian wine, which was also imported into south-east Britain. Wine was poured from bronze flagons into cups or bowls. Beer was drunk from tankards or drinking horns.

An unusual find in Orkney of mineralised human faeces, voided onto heather and bracken and then thrown into a disused well, has enabled archaeologists to investigate an everyday diet about 2,000 years ago. A great deal of meat was eaten, including venison and mutton. Any fish was the large cod, which suggests comparatively deep-sea fishing from boats with a line. Barley was used to make broth or to thicken a meat stew. Meat was often cooked in a stone trough inset into the floor; the cook kept the water boiling by inserting stones which had been heated in the fire.

That Scotland became Celtic, and, unlike the rest of Britain, remained entirely so until about AD 800, was more the result of wholesale infiltration than of invasion, colonisation, or immigration. One cannot put any precise dates to this development or define its causes; one can only recognise the presence of its effects. There was, however, in about 150 BC, a large influx of Belgian Celts into south-east Britain, which spread as far as the Humber. This would have had a knock-on effect on Celtic tribes farther to the north, who in turn pressed into the agricultural land the other side of the Cheviot hills, the natural boundary which since AD 1018 has divided Scotland from England. That there were trading links between Scottish and Irish Celts at least as early as about 250 BC is now attested by the Torrs bronze pony-cap and drinking-horn terminals, prestige goods decorated in Irish style and found in south-west Scotland.

Classical writers described the Celts variously as huge and aggressive, with staring blue eyes. The historian Cornelius Tacitus (AD 56/57–c.117) picks out, among the Celtic tribes of Britain, the Caledonians for their 'red hair and big bones, proof of a Germanic origin' (*Agricola* 11. 2). Modern studies cite Scots as having a greater incidence of red or ginger hair than any other peoples in the world. This suggests a genetic tendency which, despite subsequent, and often large-scale, immigration, has survived since that time. The aggression of the Celts frightened even the Romans, ever since an incursion in 390 BC by Celts from Gaul, who charged at, and overran, the Roman army a few miles outside Rome by tactical use of their iron longswords, and then were cravenly allowed to enter the city itself without opposition. The whole of western history might have been altered had they not accepted a bribe of gold to go away, after, it was said, the Gauls had tried to use false weights to arrive at the final sum! Instead, the Romans coined a word to describe what they saw as the constant Celtic threat – it can be translated as 'state of emergency'. Celtic men gloried in their height, but not, apparently in their girth: in Transalpine Gaul, a young man whose waist size exceeded the standard length of belt faced punishment. Short beards were often worn, though Julius Caesar describes the Britons as shaving every part of their body except the head and upper lip. Moustaches were so long and straggly that it was said that their owners drank as though through a strainer. Fighting men smeared their hair with a thick wash of lime, and then drew it back into spikes so stiff that they could pierce a falling apple. Some Celts fought naked, not in bravado, but because they thought they thus had magical protection. It is from Julius Caesar (100–44 BC) that we first learn that 'all the Britons stain themselves with woad, which gives them a blue effect, and makes them look more frightening in battle' (*Gallic Wars* V. 14). Celts in general seemed to fear nothing, except that the sky might fall on their heads.

Women could be equally formidable. Many of them, in black robes and with their hair dishevelled, brandishing torches, mingled with the army drawn up on the beach at Anglesey to face the invading Romans in AD 60. They were not averse to taking part, either:

> A cohort of foreigners could not face a single Gaul who calls up his wife to help him. She is very powerful, with flashing blue eyes. When the veins of her neck stand out, and she gnashes her teeth and swings her vast white forearms, her punches, mixed with kicks, are like shots from a torsion catapult.
>
> Ammianus Marcellinus, *Res Gestae* XV. 12. 1

When the Celtic Ambrones were forced to retreat by a Roman army under Marius in 101 BC, the women of the tribe defended their wagons with swords and hatchets, and set upon their own men as traitors as well as the Romans as enemies.

In other respects too the Celts operated an equal opportunities society to an extent unknown elsewhere in the ancient world. Both classical sources and Irish and Welsh laws suggest that women could own and manage property. Married couples operated a kind of joint bank account. Each put into a pool a certain sum, which was added up each year and the profits assessed and retained. If a husband died, his widow took back her contribution, and all the joint profits. On marriage in Wales, the husband or his family paid the price of the wife's virginity before the first night, unlike the practice in Roman and Germanic societies, where it was not handed over until the following morning. There is some evidence, too, that a woman had the right to choose her own husband; certainly she could not legally be married without her consent. Divorce was straightforward, and no stigma was attached to a divorced wife. This does not mean that there was no sympathy for a wronged spouse. When Cartimandua, queen of the Brigantes in Britain, tired of her husband Venutius and took her armour-bearer as her official consort, there was a revolution against her. She was only extricated from an exceedingly dangerous situation by the intervention of Roman troops to whom she had appealed for help, but Venutius got back his position.

Julius Caesar describes the Britons as practising a form of collective marriage: 'Ten or twelve men share wives; this is particularly the case of brothers with brothers and fathers with sons. But children born of such an arrangement are reckoned to belong to the home which the woman first entered as a virgin' (*Gallic Wars* V. 14). Cassius Dio describes a similar custom among the Caledonians and Maeatae in Scotland, with the difference that the children were brought up communally. He also tells of an occasion, which can be dated to AD 209, when Julia Domna, wife of the Roman emperor Septimius Severus, jokingly took to task the wife of a Caledonian called Argentocoxus for the habits of her tribe in having free sexual intercourse. The lady drew herself up and replied, 'We fulfil our natural desires in a better way than you Romans. We freely have sex with the best men: you give yourselves in private to the worst' (*Roman History* LXXVII. 16. 5).

British women not only owned property; they also ran their own businesses and pursued their own careers. This was the case too in Gaul, where there were women butchers, chemists, doctors, and wine-sellers. Of the Celts in Britain, Tacitus stated, 'There is no sexual discrimination where authority is concerned' (*Agricola* 16. 1). He was speaking particularly of Boudica, leader of the Iceni and of the Celtic revolt in Britain against Rome in AD 60. Cassius Dio describes her as very tall, with a fierce look in her eye, and a strident voice. She had a mass of tawny hair down to her hips, and a huge gold torque around her neck. She invariably wore a multi-coloured tunic under a thick cloak fastened with a brooch.

The length of Boudica's hair was a symbol of her status, as was the size and nature of the torque, the neck-ring of gold or bronze, or some-times of silver, worn by men as well as women. Tacitus refers to a cloak, fastened by a brooch or a thorn, being standard dress among German Celts, to the extent that only the wealthy could afford to wear anything underneath it. Be that as it may, the standard undergarment for both sexes was a linen tunic, in the case of women falling to the ankles. Men commonly wore woollen trousers, probably introduced by horsemen from the east. Tunics were often dyed in various colours. Sheep of dif-ferent colouring, black, grey, reddish, tan, and brown, as well as white, were bred for their natural wool, or for producing wool which in the form of yarn or cloth readily took dyes. Patterns, much like the Scottish tartan, were also woven. Skins were employed as leather or, complete with the original hair or wool, for bags, caps, or capes. Very popular with British Celts, and those in similar climes, was the *birrus Britannicus*, a cloak made of goats' wool, which came with its own hood attached.

Social status was indicated not only by clothing and personal adornment, but also by the decoration of everyday items such as knife-handles, pins, and mirrors – examples of hand-mirrors found in England and Scotland are so heavy that they must have been held up by a slave or ladies' maid. Celtic art is distinctive for the whorls and other intricacies of its geometrical designs, often achieved with the help of compasses. These appear on mirror backs, plaques, brooches, vases and pots, scabbards, mounts, and bronze bowls, as well as on jew-ellery and other artefacts of many kinds. The technique continued in Britain until the Dark Ages which began in about AD 400, and sur-vives today on the stone crosses and inscribed slabs of that period which can be seen in Scotland.

The people of the 'Urnfield Culture', the forerunners of the mid-European Celts, generally cremated their dead and placed the remains in urns which they buried in flat cemeteries. The Celts themselves favoured inhumation in graves or pits, or in slab-lined cists, with grave-goods demonstrating the status of the individual. While few such burial sites have actually been unearthed in Scotland, they are still there for the finding. In March 2003, a mechanical digger on a building site near the town centre of Alloa, Clackmannanshire, eased the lid off a cist containing the skeleton probably of a local tribal chief. His head was on a stone pillow. He was fully clothed, and had his sword in his hand; around him were toe-rings, ornate copper pins, and glass beads.

The Scottish Highlands are generally regarded as the region to the west and north of the Highland Line, a geological fault which runs from Dumbarton to Stonehaven. A tribal society of a kind, speaking a Celtic language, survived in the Highlands and Western Isles of Scotland until the middle of the eighteenth century; the language itself, which in the sixteenth century was spoken by about a quarter of the population, still survives perilously today, with about 70,000 speakers. Gaelic has, however, now been given legal status as an official language, and is being revivified, with a national board, new (state-subsidised) literature, and regular radio and television programmes.

The structure of Celtic society in Scotland at the beginning of the first millennium AD is likely to have reflected that of Gaul and Ireland. The king or chief came from one of the aristocratic landowning families whose representatives were part of the ruling council. A woman could be elected or accepted as chief, and also war leader, as in the cases of Boudica and Cartimandua. Tacitus refers to members of the tribe of the Brigantes, led by a woman, setting fire to a Roman settlement and storming a camp. The ruling class also included the religious men: the druids, seers, and bards. Beneath them were the property-owning farmers, whose wealth was measured in cattle, and the craftsmen. There was a further class represented by lesser farmers, minor craftsmen, and the landless but still free, who were not consulted about anything. Slaves, who might be prisoners-of-war, debtors, or men or women captured abroad and bought from slave traders, had no rights. This did not prevent a female slave from representing a unit of value, as was the case in Ireland.

The religious practices of the Celts were, like other religions with which the Celts later identified themselves, a strong influence on the society they served. The druids were the priests of the Celtic religious and supernatural beliefs. Their training lasted about 20 years, and they alone communicated with the innumerable gods and goddesses of the

Celtic pantheon, and interpreted their wishes. They were also the wise men of the community, human storehouses of oral knowledge and its practical application to such subjects as astronomy and the calendar, and of the practice of law and the administration of justice. They observed the growth of the sacred mistletoe, and when the time was right, climbed the oak to garner it with a sickle. They supervised and actively participated in sacrifices, both of animals (bulls, pigs, and dogs were the most common choices) and of humans, who were often captives. According to Julius Caesar, druids paid no taxes and usually refrained from anything to do with war. Once a year, there was a druids' convention at what was regarded as the very centre of Gaul, where civil disputes were aired and settled. Caesar adds that the druidical rules of life were discovered in Britain and transferred to Gaul, and that those who wished to study them most exhaustively travelled to Britain to do so.

Seers, like the druids, were supposed to have the powers of prophecy, and studied their art for 12 years. They also interpreted sacrifices and the behaviour of natural phenomena. Bards not only declaimed at public occasions and entertainments, but also composed satirical and ceremonious verse. Though opinions are divided as to whether there were female druids, there were certainly female seers. As the emperor Alexander Severus (AD 205–35) prepared for war against the Germanic Alamanni, a Gallic prophetess warned him that he should not hope for victory, nor should he trust his own soldiers. The following year he, and his mother, were murdered in Mainz during a mutiny fomented by one of his staff officers.

Whether or not there was a separate warrior class among the Celts, war and fighting were inherent in their culture. In addition to the necessary campaigns to win new territories and settle problems of overpopulation, or to resist incursions by other tribes bent on the same course, or to oppose invasions by those such as the Romans, there was a tradition of fighting as a sport, in the same league as hunting, despite the risk of death. Tribal wars were commonplace, and contributed to the ease with which Julius Caesar completed his conquest of Gaul. Irish literature abounds with tales of the *fianna*, roving bands of teenage aristocratic warriors whose activities were regarded with much indulgence. These stories frequently allude to single combat, as a means especially of achieving prestige. The challenge to single combat was also at times a standard battle tactic reflecting the Homeric age. It was frowned upon by the Romans, who preferred to win by deploying massed ranks of disciplined legionaries. There are, however, between 361 and 222 BC, three recorded instances of a Roman leader defeating his Celtic opponent in single combat.

Celtic mercenaries feature in numerous campaigns in classical times, to the extent that it has been suggested that no eastern king went to war without them, such was their reputed prowess and the fear they inspired. In 277 BC Ptolemy II, king of Egypt, hired 4,000 Gallic troops, who plotted to take over the country. He confined them on an uninhabited island, where they killed each other or starved to death. Celtic mercenaries fought on both sides in 274 BC when Pyrrhus of Epirus (319–272 BC) invaded Macedonia and deposed its king, Antigonus. Gauls and Iberian cavalry fought for the Carthaginian forces against Rome throughout the Punic Wars in the third century BC, in spite of the Gallic reputation for treachery. Celtic auxiliaries featured in many successful Roman army campaigns. Julius Caesar was so impressed by the Gallic cavalry he fought against in Gaul that he recruited a large contingent of them for his war against Pompey in 49 BC. Celt fought Celt at the battle of Mons Graupius, when in AD 84 Agricola threw his Batavian and Tungrian infantry into the front line against the massed ranks of the Caledonians. In much the same way, and maybe not so far away either, Celtic highland detachments fought for the Hanoverian army against the highland forces of Charles Edward Stuart (AD 1720–88) at Culloden in 1746. And on that day, the prince fatally attempted to succeed by employing the traditional Celtic battle tactic, the all-out infantry charge, against the Hanoverian artillery.

Celts fought noisy battles. They blew horns and trumpets, the latter of a form unique to the Celts, the carnyx, which towered above the massed ranks of men – a bronze boar's head from one of these was found in a peat bog in Banffshire in 1916. They shouted war-cries, they sang, they howled, they screamed imprecations, they leaped up and down, they beat their shields or shook them above their heads. Then they charged, yelling all the time. Traditionally, the Celts used as war machines fast, light, two-horse chariots, carrying a driver and a fighting man. Chiefs were often buried with their chariot. A rare instance of a burial of a chief actually in his chariot was unearthed in 2003 in east

Yorkshire (territory of the tribe of the Parisi, who originated in north-ern Gaul), in the course of a major motorway upgrading scheme. The vehicle, dating to between 500 and 400 BC, had spoked wheels 1m in diameter, with iron rims fused onto them when the metal cooled. By the middle of the first century BC, such chariots had on the continent of Europe largely been superseded by cavalry, to the extent that their employment as what was to the Romans a secret weapon caused con-fusion among Julius Caesar's troops when he invaded Britain.

> First they drive all over the place, hurling missiles and causing conster-nation in the ranks from fear of the horses and by the noise of the wheels. Then, when they have got in between the squadrons of caval-ry, they jump down from their chariots and fight on foot. Meanwhile the drivers withdraw gradually from the conflict and park the chariots where the warriors have a ready means of retreat to their own lines if they are hard pressed by a mass of enemy troops. Thus they exercise, in a real situation, the mobility of cavalry and the steadfastness of infantry. By training and daily practice they become so efficient that they can control their charging horses down the steepest slopes, rein them in, and suddenly turn them.
>
> Caesar, *Gallic Wars* IV. 33

The Caledonians tried similar tactics against the Roman invaders at the battle of Mons Graupius 140 years later, but the Romans now took lit-tle notice.

Equally disconcerting even to Roman insensibilities was the Celtic tradition of decapitating their enemies and attaching the heads to the bridles of their horses or nailing them up in their homes or in sanctu-aries. Prize specimens were embalmed in cedar-oil and kept in display chests. A battle scene from Trajan's Column (AD 113) depicts an auxil-iary infantryman, who would almost certainly have been of Celtic ori-gin, holding the severed head of an enemy in his teeth. It has been sug-gested that the practice originally had some mystic significance, perhaps to do with enslaving the ghost of the owner of the head. That some symbolism was attached to severed heads is suggested by the discovery of numerous decapitated skeletons in Sculptor's Cave in the cliffs on the Moray Firth, a site which, to judge from symbols carved at the entrance, retained some ritual significance until around AD 600.

As crafts became more sophisticated and mass production was introduced, particularly of iron objects and pottery, so trade increased and urban development occurred around centres of industry and commerce. This happened from Spain right across central Europe, and in Britain on the east and south-east coasts. Scotland remained largely untouched by such advances until the thirteenth century AD when, in return for what was not produced at home, merchants exported the surplus from a subsistence economy, primarily fleeces, wool, skins and hides, and fish. The northern region was also susceptible to geological and climatic changes. A volcanic eruption in Iceland in 1159 BC caused a proliferation of vast clouds of dust. These brought increased rain, cooler weather, and shorter growing seasons. Whole communities, it is thought, migrated to the Lowlands. Living room and agricultural land were obtained by wholesale forest clearances in central and southern Scotland.

In such conditions, and especially where there was now a shortage of wood for building, something more substantial and secure was often required to meet the requirements of a growing rural population, at a time also when borders were ill-defined and tribal feelings could run high. Celtic homes on the European mainland were traditionally in the form of long-houses. In Britain and Ireland they were round, with conical thatched roofs; those in south-east Scotland often had dry-stone walls, with an internal ring of posts capable of supporting an upper, attic, floor as well as the roof. Hill-fort settlements of roundhouses were established, sometimes initially within a non-defensive series of banks and ditches. Often these settlements were later extended or were rebuilt in a different form. Defensive measures consisted of wooden palisades or dry-stone walls 18ft (6m) high, laced with timbers thrust through spaces in the wall. Vitrified forts, in which the timbers had been subjected to fierce heat, were once thought to have been fired deliberately to fuse the stones and earth for strength. Practical experiments have now revealed that such treatment would have weakened the wall. Because of the intensity of heat needed, it has been concluded that these walls were deliberately set on fire as symbolic and dramatic demonstrations of the destruction of the power of the previous local regime.

A wheel-house was a circular home designed and constructed for more exposed coastal areas such as Shetland and the Western Isles. It is so called because the stone projections from the centre, supporting a solid circle of masonry, resemble the spokes of a wheel. The lower part of the house was sunk into a pit. The entrance was reached by an underground tunnel topped with stone slabs and covered with turf. Above ground was the conical roof of wood and thatch.

A souterrain (also known as an earth-house or a weem) was an underground tunnel lined with timber or stone whose entrance was often in a wooden or stone roundhouse. It was probably used for storage.

An ingenious method of defence was incorporated in the crannog, a timber and thatch roundhouse built on an artificial island or on piles sunk into the bed of a lake, and reached by a narrow causeway or by dug-out canoe. Crannogs are confined almost exclusively to Ireland and Scotland. They were prestige establishments, often constructed of alder or oak, which have lasting properties under such conditions. Some, built in about 500 BC, were occupied continuously for 400 years. Others were in use during the first and second centuries AD. This type of dwelling survived in Scotland until the eighteenth century.

Brooding over the landscape, and unique to Scotland, were the brochs. Remains have been discovered of about 500 of these mastodons of the builder's craft. They stood as high as a four-storey block of modern flats, and were 50–65ft (15–20m) in diameter. Most are concentrated at the north-east extremity of the mainland, and in the Northern and Western Isles, but some have been found in the south and west. A broch is a circular dry-stone tower with no openings on the outside except a narrow entrance. The walls, built round a circular courtyard, are about 16ft (5m) thick, with living accommodation in galleries inside, reached by stairs. Hot air from a hearth on the first floor circulated through vents and along the galleries.

All the brochs were built between about 200 BC and AD 150. Their standard design suggests that they were constructed by teams of travelling broch builders. Some are encircled at ground level by a cluster of stone-built homes of lesser folk, like piglets huddling round a sow.

The brochs offered an effective way of countering the northern winters and the rain and hail which are driven almost horizontally by the wind at any time of the Scottish year. They were also undoubtedly statements of authority and power. Whether or not they had also a defensive purpose, they would have presented a formidable sight to any potential invaders crossing the North Sea from Scandinavia, which in the end did not happen until the eighth century AD.

When the invasion of Scotland did come, in the first century AD, it was from the south, and on foot. Except for a voyage of discovery which took in Orkney, the Romans never got farther north than Inverness. It was the single failure of the rulers and senate and people of Rome consciously to extend the Roman empire by force.

2 Italy, including places mentioned in later chapters

2

THE ROMANS AND THEIR WORLD

The Romans, too, worshipped a multiplicity of gods and goddesses, many of whom in due course were identified with their Celtic counterparts. Janus, however, who gave his name to what became the first month in the Roman calendar, is unknown in any mythology other than that of the Romans. He was the god of beginnings and of openings, such as the door of a house. The first hour of each day was sacred to him, and he received the first state sacrifice of the year. His double-headed image, facing in different directions, as does a door, appeared on the first Roman round coin in bronze, the basic *as*, in about 338 BC, in republican times. Rome was originally a monarchy. The first historical king, Numa Pompilius, decreed in about 600 BC that the gates of the temple of Janus in the north-eastern corner of the forum should remain wide open when the nation was at war. According to the historian Livy (59 BC–AD 17), they were closed only twice between then and the times in which he lived.

War was embedded in the Roman consciousness. Out of civil war came the mythological beginnings of the city and its foundation by Romulus on 21 April 753 BC – the Romans were as proud of the occasion as they were precise about its date. Another tradition traces the line of Romulus back to Aeneas, son of a mortal father and the goddess Venus. Aeneas was a hero of the Trojan War, which archaeological evidence places towards the end of the thirteenth century BC. He is said to have landed at the mouth of the river Tiber, which ran through Latium. Latinus, king of Latium, offered Aeneas his daughter in marriage, much to the fury of another local king, Turnus, who went to war against the Latins. Aeneas obtained the support of the Etruscans, and won the battle, killing Turnus in the process in single combat.

The Roman civilisation, which drew on ancient Greece for much of its culture, lasted for some 1,200 years. The Romans were supremely superstitious and largely devoid of humour, traits possibly derived from their influential neighbours, the Etruscans, who worshipped a pantheon of gloomy gods. The Romans were also ostentatious, ruthless, calculatingly brutal even by the standards of the ancient world, dedicated to law and organisation, and devoted to a system of empire which brought benefits to its inhabitants as long as they toed the Roman line. They were past masters at developing other people's ideas, becoming in the process skilled architects, builders, engineers, sculptors, and craftsmen. They were also, as far as the upper classes were concerned, inherently idle, because the economy was based on slavery. Their armies, sometimes supported by auxiliary troops and cavalry, brought tactical manoeuvring and military discipline to a fine art. The reformed calendar introduced by Julius Caesar in 46 BC is, with minor adjustments over its earlier years, the one still in use today.

The Romans adapted the Greek alphabet to their own purposes, and bequeathed it to the world. Their basic alphabet had 21 characters – Y and Z were introduced later for words borrowed from the Greek, and J, U, and W were added in the Middle Ages. One-third of the English language is based on the Latin that the Romans spoke and in which they wrote. The influence of their literature (especially epic, lyric, and elegiac poetry, and elegant prose) is such that without it there would have been virtually no English or European literature before about AD 1800. Such was the precision with which points of science, theology, philosophy, architecture, medicine, and law could be expressed in Latin that it remained the language of scholarship in western Europe throughout the Middle Ages and the Renaissance.

From the beginning of the first century AD, Latin was the official language throughout the Roman empire, and the lingua franca of the administration, the army, and centralised trade. It was also a written language, with a regulated spelling, and there were various acceptable forms of writing it, according to the circumstances. Though the Celtic dialect spoken in Britain had similarities with Latin, it was rarely written down, and thus there was little incentive for Latin-speaking invaders or settlers to learn it.

Scotland was, however, subjected to other outside influences. The predominant Celtic dialect, brought by the Dál Riata from Ireland, came to be Scottish Gaelic, so different from Gallo-Brittonic that it could not be understood by the native Picts. By the eleventh century AD Gaelic was in use throughout Scotland, only to give way in the south towards the end of the century to Norman French and then to the dialect of northern English which became Scots.

In this linguistic maelstrom, Latin continued along its distinctive course. Queen Margaret of Scotland (1046–93), later St Margaret, spoke Hungarian, French, English, and Latin, but never mastered Gaelic. Robert the Bruce (1274–1329) would have spoken Gaelic, Scots, and Norman French, and understood Latin. The Declaration of Arbroath (1320), the rightly celebrated national plea to the pope to recognise him as king of Scotland and to lift from him the sentence of excommunication, is written in rhythmical Latin prose. Early histories of Scotland by John of Fordun (c.1384), Walter Bower (c.1441), John Major (1521), and Hector Boece (1526) were written in Latin, following the influence of European scholarship. James I (1567–1625), James VI of Scotland, complained bitterly that his tutors forced him to speak Latin before he could speak Scots. His principal tutor, George Buchanan (1506–82), had been Latin tutor to James's mother, Mary Queen of Scots (1542–87), and wrote in Latin a scurrilous exposition of her private life (1571). Buchanan, a humanist scholar, also wrote in Latin several plays, two of them translated from the Greek, a corpus of poetry, metrical versions of the Psalms, and a 20-volume history of Scotland. Latin continued to be regarded in some quarters as a proper basis of literary communication until the advent of the Scottish Enlightenment in the eighteenth century.

From the beginning of the fifteenth century, however, Scottish parliamentary legislation was in Scots, rather than Latin, and by the end of the century Scots had virtually replaced Latin as the principal language of records. Even so, it was in 1605 laid down that among the qualifications of a prospective judge must be the ability to argue in Latin about a legal text, and Latin was not finally ousted as the language for Scottish legal deeds until the nineteenth century.

To the Romans are owed the principles of impartial justice and trial by jury. Scottish law, unlike English law, has a basis in Roman law. Alexander Bayne, elected in 1722 Edinburgh University's first professor of law, observed, 'We consider the Roman laws which are not disconform to our own fixed Laws and Customs, to be our own Law.' Lord

Kames (1696–1782), the Scottish judge, took a similar view: 'Our law is grafted on that of Old Rome. The Roman law is illustrious for its equitable rules, affording great scope for acute reasoning.'

The last king of Rome was ejected in 510 BC. Rome and its empire was still nominally a republic in 55 BC, when Julius Caesar embarked on the first Roman invasion of Britain. Rome was never, however, a true democracy as envisaged by the Greeks. The Latin term *res publica* can be translated as 'state' or 'commonwealth', but in its effect it was rather a political concept embracing oligarchy, autocracy, and a modicum of democracy. At its head were the two consuls, with equal powers, elected for one year only. At its heart was the senate, described by a visiting diplomat as an 'assembly of kings'. In its procedures and political ideals incorporating open debate, it resembled the modern American senate, except that its members were appointed.

There were four other assemblies, of which the most significant was the *comitia centuriata*, which elected senior officials, made declarations of war and peace, approved legislation, and had the final say in cases of execution or exile until these functions were transferred to the courts. It comprised 193 'centuries', to which the electorate (that is all Roman citizens) were allocated according to their wealth. Any ballot by centuries, however, was rigged in that 98 of the votes, a majority, were cast by the 18 centuries of equestrians (or knights), second in influence only to the senators, and the 80 centuries representing the upper of five property bands.

There were further divides between the patricians, members of a closed group of noble families, and the *plebs*, the common people, and between those who regarded themselves as aristocrats and the rest. There was even a derogatory term, '*novus homo*' (upstart, literally a new man), to describe the first of a family to achieve public office. Rights for the *plebs* had, however, been achieved over the years by passive resistance, collective bargaining, and the threat, sometimes carried out, of withdrawing themselves and their labour to hold a public protest. From 367 BC one consulship could be held by a plebeian. There was a plebeian parliament, the *concilium plebis*, with its own elected officers. A *tribunus plebis*, tribune of the people, had extraordinary powers. A government official could annul any act of a colleague of similar status: the tribune could hold up almost any state business, even a resolution of the senate, by pronouncing a veto.

In such a heterogeneous system, it was inevitable that there were tensions, which increased with the demands of governing a burgeoning empire. There was no built-in release for these tensions, either at home or abroad, except violence. Tiberius Gracchus (168–133 BC), tribune of the people in 133 BC, put forward a package of proposals designed to combat injustice and greed, among which was the redistribution among smallholders of land in Italy acquired by the state. Instead of submitting it to the senate, he raised it in the *comitia tributa*, the assembly open to all citizens, where it was bound to succeed. A commission was appointed to administer the scheme. When, after some 75,000 smallholdings had been created, funds ran short, Tiberius proposed in the *comitia tributa* that revenue from the newly annexed kingdom of Pergamum should be diverted to the commission's use. A furious senate had now been outflanked twice. State officials could not be prosecuted while in office, but they could be brought to book afterwards for acts committed during their term. Tiberius coolly took an unprecedented and arguably illegal step, and announced his candidature for the tribuneship for a second year running. This was too much for the senate. A group of its members broke up an electioneering meeting which Tiberius was addressing, and beat him to death with cudgels and stools.

His flamboyant younger brother, Gaius Gracchus (*c.*159–121 BC), was also a victim of senatorial terrorism, though this time the senate had been careful to arm itself with a *senatus consultum ultimum*, which gave backing to senior officials to take action against those who were believed to be endangering the stability of the state. Gaius lost the election for tribune of the people in 121 BC when the senate put up against him a straw candidate with a fake programme of reforms even more liberal than his. Gaius's supporters held a rally on the Aventine Hill. Some of them, unwisely, were armed. A citizen levy augmented by soldiers was raised to disperse the demonstrators. Gaius took evasive action and ordered his slave to stab him to death in a nearby grove. It is said that in the subsequent mayhem, 3,000 of his supporters were put in jail, and strangled.

Political bribery and manipulation of the polls were common practices. In 51 and 50 BC, Julius Caesar, from his command in Gaul, resorted to lavish bribery of a tribune of the people, and also of one of the consuls, to ensure that any legislation was vetoed which was not in his personal interests. In 49, however, he was ordered to lay down his command. When he refused to do, the senate announced an official state of emergency. Caesar, faced with a choice of losing his command, and becoming liable for prosecution for acts committed while he was consul in 59 BC, or leading his army on Rome, elected to cross the river Rubicon with his troops, thus becoming an enemy of the state. The subsequent civil war lasted for four years. It changed the course of history, and also contributed to Caesar's death at the height of his achievements. Caesar was a primarily a political animal. He dealt out brutality and mercy in equal measures, whichever suited his ends at the time. His attitude to Romans who fought against him was to spare them on the first occasion they were captured. Among the senior officers to whom he granted immunity after the battle of Pharsalus in 48 BC was one Marcus Junius Brutus (c.85–42 BC), son of Caesar's mistress Servilia. Brutus was subsequently a leader of the conspiracy which caused Caesar's assassination in 44 BC.

After his consulship, Caesar had been appointed governor of Gaul. He went through the motions of resolving some of the political differences with the Celtic tribes there by diplomacy, then acquired the province by force, and by shows of arms and making examples of those who broke their apparent word. After wiping out the entire fighting complement of the Nervii in 57 BC, he told the old men, women, and children of the tribe, who had surrendered to him, to go home, and ordered that they should not be molested by their neighbours. Then he forced his way into the hill-top stronghold of the Aduatuci, whose warriors had tried to deceive him by only partially decommissioning their weapons, and sold off the whole town and its 53,000 inhabitants to the slave dealers. He responded to rebels against his authority who holed themselves up in Uxellodunum in 51 BC by amputating the hands of all those who had borne arms in the revolt.

There was no Roman mercy at all in AD 132 when the Second Jewish War erupted, it is believed because of a prohibition on certain traditional practices and an insensitive proposal by the emperor Hadrian (AD 76–138) to turn the holy site of Jerusalem into a Hellenistic city. In the course of it, 580,000 men are said to have been killed, and so many of the survivors, including women and children, were sold to the dealers that there was a surplus on the international slave market and prices slumped. At the war's end Hadrian had what remained of Jerusalem ploughed into the ground, and a new city erected, which Jews were forbidden to enter. The Roman province of Judaea was now renamed Syria Palaestina, or Palestine.

Such insensitivity was a form of arrogance, which had its roots in the religious traditions and fragmented beliefs of the Romans, many of whose gods and goddesses were borrowed from Greek mythology. To the Romans, religion was a contractual arrangement. In return for services offered by way of prayer and sacrifice, benefits could be obtained, on a national or personal basis. The sacrifice need not be an animal, as long as it represented life in some form, such as fruit, cheese, wine, milk, or cakes.

The Romans shared with the Celts a belief in animism. The Celts had their sanctuaries and holy islands, sacred groves and trees, springs, bogs, and lakes, and even ritual wells and shafts. The Romans took this to extremes, and invested not only natural phenomena with supernatural properties, but also animals, household furniture, and stones. From the Etruscans they inherited their preoccupation with omens, to the extent that no action by the state or conduct of public business could be undertaken without recourse to them. The taking of auspices (literally 'signs from birds', for example their number and the direction in which they were flying) was such a standard procedure that armies on the march or navies at sea took along a portable auspice-kit, comprising a cage of sacred chickens, which, at the appropriate juncture, were offered pieces of cake. If they ate them and dropped bits of grain from their beaks, that was a good sign. If they refused to eat, the omens were bad. Such was the case when Claudius Pulcher arrived in Sicily to take up his command against the Carthaginians in 249 BC. His response was to throw the chickens into the sea, remarking that if they would not eat, they could drink instead. In the ensuing naval débâcle, 93 Roman ships and their crews were captured by the Carthaginians.

Julius Caesar was notoriously sceptical about omens. When an augur announced the bad news that a sacrificial beast had no heart at all for him to examine, Caesar is said to have 'replied that the omens would be more favourable when he wished them to be, and that it should not be any wonder that an animal lacked a heart' (Suetonius, *Life of Julius Caesar* 77). On the morning of his assassination, however, initially he bowed to his wife's and the official augurs' interpretations of her nightmares and promised to stay at home. He was then persuaded by one of the conspirators who was a close personal friend that if this was indeed an unlucky day on which to conduct the senate's business, he should at least, in his position as head of state, make an appearance and formally adjourn the meeting.

There were signs which were invoked and signs which appeared unexpectedly. The latter usually gave warnings of problems ahead. Lightning was a common sign, more ominous if a bolt hit something or someone – in 114 BC a vestal virgin was struck by lightning. Thunder was regarded more favourably. Cato the Elder (234–149 BC), elected to the office of censor in 184 BC, took his responsibilities as guardian of public morals very seriously, confessing that he never embraced his wife unless it was thundering, but adding that he was happy when it did. Formal political business could be halted, or legislation rejected, if the omens were unfavourable. Marcus Bibulus (d. *c.*32 BC), Caesar's unfortunate consular colleague in 59 BC, sent messages to the senate from his home stating that as he was sure the omens would be unfavourable, he was watching for them. An epileptic fit on the part of a member of an assembly was enough for the proceedings to be cancelled; parties with interests that this should happen were known to throw fake seizures.

The religion of the state was under the direction of the *pontifex maximus*, who was also in charge of the calendar and supervised the observance of days which were regarded as unlucky and therefore unsuitable for public business. Members of the Pontifical College, the senior of four such bodies, were the administrators and organisers of religious affairs, and especially of the numerous religious festivals. The counterpart of the *pontifex maximus* for worship in the home was the head of the family. The household had its own gods, *lares* and *penates*, represented by tiny statuettes which lived in their own cupboards. There were rituals and deities for almost everything, including the various stages of child development. After death, the spirit of the corpse (even in the case of cremation a single bone was retained and put in the ground) joined all the other spirits of the dead, the *manes*, to whom worship and appeasement were regularly offered. Agricultural rituals and rural festivals occupied the countryman's year from April to the end of December, often accompanied by much jollification.

Superstition and belief in supernatural powers pervaded if not controlled every aspect of Roman life, even the army. The public games had their origins as adjuncts to religious festivals, and their religious character was maintained. Just as the slightest unintentional deviation from the prescribed ritual of sacrifice meant that a new ceremony had to be performed from the beginning, so the games could be extended by one, two, or three days, or totally replayed, if anything untoward happened. According to Caesar's contemporary and intellectual equal, the lawyer and politician Cicero (106–43 BC), this could be a gladiator giving up the fight, a flautist suddenly stopping in the middle of a bar, a boy letting go of the ceremonial chariot carrying the images of the gods or dropping the reins, or the aedile slipping up over a word of an announcement.

The Latin word *ludi* (games) covers two forms of entertainment. *Ludi scaenici* refers to theatrical performances. Roman drama developed from the Greek but had on the whole nothing like the enduring quality or status of the plays of the great tragic and comic dramatists of Greece such as Aeschylus (525–456 BC), Sophocles (496–406 BC), Euripides (*c*.484–407 BC), and Aristophanes (*c*.445–*c*.380 BC). Shakespeare, however, based his *Comedy of Errors* on the *Menaechmi* of the Roman playwright Plautus (254–184 BC). A later writer of comedies was Terence, a former slave, probably from Africa, who was educated by his owner, and then given his freedom. He is said to have been drowned in a shipwreck in 159 BC at the age of 26, on a trip to Greece to look for new plots to use. His *The Mother-in-Law* had three first nights at separate games. On the first occasion, in the seemingly inappropriate setting of a staging of funeral games, the performance was abandoned when the audience called instead for the appearance they had been promised of a tight-rope walker. Half way through the second, someone had announced that the gladiators were about to begin. The audience surged out in a body.

The custom-built circuses and amphitheatres housed the *ludi circenses*, a term which covered both chariot races and gladiatorial shows. The Circus Maximus, built in 329 BC, was 635m long. Over 200,000 spectators at a time could watch the hair-raising 4,000-metre dashes, seven times round the track, and bet on the results. The drivers were slaves, but also professional sportsmen, whose skill, nerve, and split-second timing could earn them fame and fortune.

The gladiatorial combat was originally borrowed from Etruscan religious tradition, and made its first Roman appearance as part of a performance of funeral games in 264 BC. Man was pitted against man, then men against beasts, then wild animals, even sea mammals, against each other. The Colosseum could hold 87,000 spectators. At its inaugural show in AD 80, which lasted 100 days, 5,000 wild beasts and 4,000 tame animals were slaughtered on the first day to please the baying crowds. Cicero, while condoning the courage and self-control needed by the gladiator, the result of training and mental conditioning, questioned whether a cultured person could derive any pleasure from watching a man torn to pieces by a beast, or an animal hunted down to death. Sometimes the amphitheatre was flooded for a full-scale naval battle, the ships being manned by condemned criminals or prisoners-of-war. Caesar instituted the custom of constructing an artifical lake for the purpose, on which he pitted two fleets, each propelled by 10,000 oarsmen. Wherever in the empire there was a considerable concentration of Roman soldiers, such as in a legionary fortress, an amphitheatre was built for their entertainment, and probably also for use as a training ground. Traces relating to an amphitheatre have now been discovered in Scotland, at Newstead, which would have served the permanent garrison of 1,000 troops, up to 5,000 at one time in temporary camps nearby, and men stationed in smaller forts in the region.

Attendance at the games was free for Roman citizens. In the time of Caesar, and later that of Augustus, 150,000 of those on or below the poverty line received free grain, which they ground into flour to make bread. The population of Rome at that time has been estimated at about a million, plus about 300,000 slaves. As in other societies of the ancient and modern world, slavery was built into the fabric of the economy. In the case of the Roman empire, when the calls of Christianity, which preached not so much abolition as benevolence, caused a reduction in the supply of slaves, the economy, never the strongest element of the constitution, began to disintegrate. Freed slaves joined the free-born poor in struggling for existence. The only acceptable career opportunities for upper-class men were in the army, politics, or law. Management posts in almost all the professions, including the civil service, were held by emancipated slaves, usually from abroad. The army was the means by which Rome preserved its existence and acquired its empire: the empire was the means by which the army was maintained. By deploying its citizen army, Rome went from village on the river Tiber, protecting itself against its neighbours with a scratch force of a few hundred, to world super-power in 600 years. Tactically, the Romans borrowed from the Greeks the formation of the phalanx, heavily-armed infantry (hoplites), close-packed and carrying spears, in massed lines of variable length but usually eight, later 12 or 16, rows deep. If a man in the front line fell, his place was taken by someone from the second line, and so on.

The fighting season was short, the summer months before the sowing and garnering of the harvest. At the beginning of the fourth century BC, probably as a result of the army being involved in a protracted siege of the Etruscan city of Veii in 396 BC, a system of payment was introduced as compensation for those who had to serve throughout the year. At about the same time it was realised that a radical change of arms and tactics was required to combat the Celts who had settled in the north of Italy. The Celts were taller than the Italians of the Latin League of tribes, of which Rome was a founder member and subsequently the leader. The angle of attack of their slashing longswords was from above or from the side. A more flexible line-up was introduced, with smaller units, known as maniples, operating separately. The circular hoplite shield was abandoned in favour of the long Italian body shield. Heavy javelins replaced the thrusting spears. In keeping with the Roman aptitude for adopting and adapting other people's ideas, the Spanish short stabbing sword with a 17in (43cm) double-edged blade was introduced at the beginning of the third century BC. Unlike the Greeks, Etruscans, Macedonians, Celts and Germans, the Romans wore their sword in a scabbard on the right side, to avoid opening the body to attack when they drew it. The army was divided for administrative purposes as well as for battle first into two and then into four legions, wholly drawn from Roman citizens. These were bolstered by contingents of troops from Latium and other Italian peoples who had surrendered to Rome or had been accepted as allies.

The Romans took a pragmatic attitude towards defeated peoples. They refused to deal with associations of towns or states. Each conquest was given individual treatment according to the circumstances. Some peoples were granted Roman citizenship without the right to vote, some only conditional citizenship. Some had to surrender part of their land, which became state property, or was divided up into estates or smallholdings for Roman citizens depending on their influence, or earmarked as a new colony. Colonies helped to meet the growing population's need for land. By settling its own citizens or Latin allies along significant land routes or at strategic coastal points, Rome was able to consolidate its control of the region. By 171 BC a growing network of roads joined Italy north to south and east to west. Defeated states were sometimes granted the privilege of trade and intermarriage with Rome, but not with each other. All provided recruits for the armed forces of Rome, either as legionaries or as auxiliaries. By 265 BC Rome had conquered the whole of the Italian peninsular south of the river Arno. In 191 BC the rest of the territory was secured by the defeat of the Celts who had settled in the valley of the Po. By 49 BC distinctions between the peoples of Italy had been erased; all were now full Roman citizens. They were also eligible to fight in the legions.

The road to total domination of Italy had not been easy. The Samnites were easy meat on the central plains of Italy, but quite a different proposition once they retired to their haunts in the mountains. In 321 BC the Romans suffered the most humiliating defeat in their whole history when the complete army, with the consuls at its head, was trapped in the Caudine Forks, a series of narrow mountain passes, and surrendered. Six hundred equestrians were handed over as hostages. The rest, headed by the consuls, stripped of their cloaks of office, were then forced to pass under the yoke, symbolising submission, while the Samnites cracked jokes and hurled insults at them. 'When they emerged from the pass, though their appearance was of men back from the grave first seeing the light of day, as they looked around at the ghastly procession, the light seemed grimmer than any death' (Livy, *History of Rome* IX. 6). The Samnite wars lasted until 290 BC. The Etruscan empire was finally dismantled in 283 BC.

Several cities had been founded in the south by settlers from Greece. Of these, the regions of Calabria and Apulia were delighted to be taken under Roman protection against hostile tribes in central Italy. Not so the city of Tarentum, which called on Pyrrhus, king of Epirus, for help. He arrived from the west coast of Greece in 280 BC with, it is said, 20,000 hoplite mercenaries, 3,000 cavalry, and a corps of elephants, which the Romans had never seen before. It was also a feat of arms between the Roman formation and the Greek phalanx, armed with pikes 16ft (5m) long overlapping each other. In 1314, Robert the Bruce defeated the English invaders at Bannockburn by equipping and arranging his spearmen in just this fashion. Pyrrhus managed to overcome the Romans at Heraclea by ingenious deployment of his elephants. A further successful encounter at Ausculum the following year was at such general cost to his own forces that he was said to have remarked that one more victory like that would be the end of him. He then took himself, what remained of his forces, and his elephants, across to Sicily.

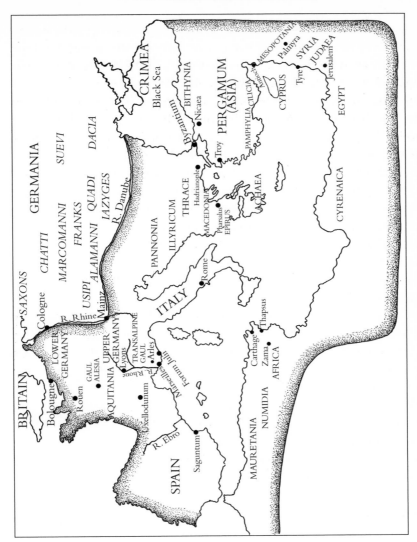

3 The Roman Empire at the death of Augustus in AD 14, with places and peoples mentioned in later chapters

The First Punic War, against Carthage, was sparked off by a diplomatic incident after there appeared to be Carthaginian interference in a domestic issue. It lasted from 264 to 241 BC, and was fought largely at sea. The Romans were not sailors by nature or inclination. A captured Carthaginian vessel provided the blueprint for a fleet of 200 quinqueremes, with three banks of oars, each pulled by five oarsmen, and carrying 120 soldiers. An ingenious swivelling attachment at the bows, which could be raised and lowered at will, enabled the troops to cross over onto the enemy ship. There were also 20 triremes, with three men to each oar, used primarily for reconnaissance. The Carthaginians finally sued for peace after there had been massive losses of manpower on both sides, and agreed to withdraw from their occupation of cities in the western part of Sicily, which became Rome's first province.

The reaction of the Carthaginians to their defeat was to increase their own empire by making inroads into the predominantly Celtic territory of Spain. They did this so successfully that Rome was forced to halt the advance by diplomatic means. The Carthaginians agreed to confine their activities to the region south of the river Ebro, with the exception of the coastal town of Saguntum, which was an ally of Rome. The Second Punic War was deliberately provoked by Hannibal (247–182 BC), who had taken over command of the Carthaginian forces in 229 BC when his father, Hamilcar, was murdered by a slave whose master he had put to death. In 218 BC Hannibal attacked and ultimately succeeded in capturing Saguntum. War was declared, a very different one from the first, and fought largely in Italy itself.

While the Romans busied themselves building another fleet, Hannibal did the impossible. He marched his army, infantry, cavalry, baggage train, and his famous elephants out of Spain, and put them across the river Rhône on boats and rafts, against fierce opposition from the local Celts. He invaded northern Italy, having found a way across the Alpine barriers, with about 20,000 infantry and 6,000 cavalry. With these, his surviving elephants, and volunteers from the Gallic Celts who had settled in the region, he outflanked one Roman division at the river Trebia, and trapped and destroyed another at Lake Trasimene. He then bypassed Rome and arrived in the south, where his 40,000 troops met the main Roman army of 16 legions, totalling about 75,000 men. By tactical use of his Celtic and Spanish infantry, African spearmen, and Celtic cavalry, Hannibal out-thought his opponents at Cannae in 216 BC, killing over 50,000 of them. Even now, Rome would not surrender. So for the next 14 years, without the resources to lay siege to the city itself, Hannibal and his army rampaged around southern Italy, while Rome scraped the barrel of its manpower to rearm itself. Slaves and serving prisoners were enlisted, and the *capite censi* (men without property, normally exempt from military service) were called up. Hannibal was finally summoned back to Carthage, and was in 202 BC defeated, elephants and all, at Zama. As part of the settlement, Carthage lost its Spanish acquisitions, and agreed not to fight anyone without permission from Rome.

The Third Punic War (149–146 BC) was engineered by Rome as a means of finally destroying the Carthaginian threat. That it lasted as long as it did was due to the heroic defence of Carthage itself. When it ended, the once-proud city, founded in about 800 BC by Phoenicians from Tyre and seat of the Carthaginian maritime empire, had been reduced to smoking rubble. The 50,000 survivors of the siege were handed over to the slave dealers.

With the acquisition of what had been Carthaginian territory in Africa, Rome was now enlarging its empire. Corsica and Sardinia had been annexed in 238 BC, the whole of Sicily in 210 BC. Spain became nominally Roman in 197 BC, but continued for many years to be home to Celtic troublemakers. Macedonia was made a province in 149 BC, and Asia Minor, having been annexed in 133 BC, was organised into provinces over the next few years. Transalpine Gaul (corresponding roughly to Provence and Languedoc) became a province in about 121 BC. During the next 70 years some 15 further territories were added to the list, including (for administrative purposes) Cisalpine Gaul (Italy north of the river Rubicon) and Gaul itself (conquered by Caesar). Each province had a Roman governor, and paid taxes to Rome. The main reasons for formalising this expansion were defence, law and order, imperialistic tendencies, lust for conquest, and profit. Bound up with the last two of these was the necessity now of maintaining and rewarding a standing army capable of operating anywhere in the known western world and in the near and middle east.

A regular legionary at the time of Caesar earned a gross wage of 225 denarii a year, which was raised by the emperor Domitian (AD 51–96) to 300 denarii. Out of this he had to pay for his food, clothing, and equipment. A soldier's rewards, and an incentive to serve, were the spoils of war, in slaves and booty. On campaign, personal booty was accumulated in an army's baggage train. At any suggestion that this might be abandoned, legionaries were in the habit of disobeying orders and ransacking the wagons for their personal property. After the battles for Alesia in 52 BC, Caesar distributed the Celtic prisoners to his troops as slaves, one per man. Advance 130 years, to about AD 80, and, according to a receipt scratched on a wooden writing tablet, an official in London bought a young female slave called Fortunata, a member of a Celtic tribe in north-east Gaul, for 600 denarii; that is, the equivalent of two years' pay for a legionary at that time.

One person can change the course of history. In Gaius Marius (157–86 BC), Lucius Cornelius Sulla (138–78 BC), and Julius Caesar, Rome had three in quick succession. Marius reorganised the army into a professional force, and rearmed it. Sulla reorganised the constitution, effectively putting the power back into the hands of the upper classes. He also introduced the terrifying process of proscription – the publication of lists of those he wanted killed, whom anyone was now at liberty to assassinate, and for a reward. Caesar, a politician *par excellence* who was also a master military strategist, secured the rest of Gaul for the empire, showed the way to Britain, extended the franchise to those of non-Roman birth, made membership of the senate more accessible, and reduced overcrowding in Rome by encouraging emigration to Roman colonies abroad. All three men presided over a republican system which was too unwieldy to last.

The army of the late republic comprised at any one time about a dozen legions each of some 5,000 men. The fighting strength of a legion consisted of ten cohorts, each originally containing six centuries of 80 men, commanded by a centurion. A legion was a miniature army, with its own craftsmen, engineers, surveyors, and other specialists, and artillery. It was supported by auxiliary troops, which included the cavalry, drawn from non-Roman allies. In addition to their weapons, cooking equipment, rations, and entrenching tools, legionaries carried their own personal gear attached to their persons or on a forked pole. Their overburdened appearance earned for them the sobriquet of Marius's Mules. Conscripts served for six years, volunteers for up to 16 years.

Caesar's initial five-year command in 58 BC was as governor of Cisalpine Gaul and Illyricum. With Celtic tribes in Gaul itself massing for trouble, a new governor of Transalpine Gaul had been appointed with orders to prosecute a war against them if necessary. He died on the way to take up his post, and Caesar was allowed by the senate to add it to his own portfolio. Thus was set in motion the train of events which led to Caesar's Gallic wars, and to Britain. The Celts in Gaul had space and natural resources. The acquisition of their territories by Rome would release some of the growing population of Italy from the physical restrictions imposed by its geography, while at the same time extending the buffer zone between Italy and the dangerous Germanic tribes east of the river Rhine. There were therefore social and economic, as well as political, justifications for his aggressive tactics.

Caesar started with four legions, which he supplemented with two more, drawn from volunteers from his own province of Cisalpine Gaul, among whom, against the rules, were non-Roman citizens from the area north of the river Po. Initially he equipped and paid these out of his own pocket. As the wars progressed he raised further legions, to the extent that in 52 and 51 BC he had 12 under his command.

Caesar's Gallic wars opened in 58 BC with a masterly win over the combined Helvetii, Boii, and Tulungi tribes. They felt threatened by their Germanic counterparts across the Rhine, and also by their Celtic neighbours, the Aedui and Sequani, and were attempting a mass migration to the west coast of Gaul. Caesar's excuse was that the Aedui and Sequani, through whose territories the march went, now felt threatened themselves, and appealed to Rome for help. In 55 BC, he learned that his cronies Crassus (c.115–53 BC) and Pompey the 'Great' (106–48 BC), consuls for that year, had secured, as well as lush post-consular pickings for themselves, a five-year extension of his own command. By then he had subdued the Suevi from across the Rhine, the Belgic federation, the western tribes of what is now Normandy and Brittany (with the help of a naval victory), and, by dubious tactics, a group of Germanic tribes who had trespassed into Gaul. It was now the moment to do something really spectacular!

He refused an offer of local river boats in which to ferry his army 400m across the Rhine to make a show of force – no Roman took a boat if he could ride or walk. Instead he had his engineers build a timber bridge. According to him, it was finished in ten days, and there seems now no serious reason to doubt this claim. He then sent his men across the bridge into Germania, where for 18 days they created as much havoc and damage as they could. Once they were back in Gaul, he had the bridge destroyed.

Though it was late in the campaign season, there was still time, he felt, and the moment was ripe, for one more glorious exploit before he retired to his province of Cisalpine Gaul for the winter recess. He would invade Britain with an expeditionary force of two legions.

4 Britain, with places mentioned in chapter 3

3

THE INVASIONS OF BRITAIN

Caesar assembled his fleet at Portus Itius (Boulogne). It comprised 80 transports rigged with a single square sail slightly forward of amidships, which he had commandeered from the coastal tribe of the Morini, and an escort of warships, driven by oars. Each transport carried a crew and 125 legionaries with their arms and personal gear. A further 18 transports, for the cavalry, were standing off 7½ miles (12km) away, prevented by the wind from making the rendezvous. Caesar ordered them to head for Ambleteuse just to the north, pick up the 500 cavalry there, and follow him as soon as they could. The main fleet sailed at about 1 a.m. on 25 August 55 BC, on a favourable wind and tide.

To the men of the Seventh Legion and those of Caesar's favourite Tenth, they were venturing into the utter unknown, and they had probably never been to sea before. Caesar's justification for the expedition was that the Celts in Britain were sending aid to the Celts in Gaul, and there is archaeological and historical evidence to support this. According to the geographer Strabo (*c.*64 BC–AD 19) there were no fewer than four regular trade routes between Gaul and southern Britain, from the river Rhine via Boulogne, from the Seine, from the Loire, and from the Garonne. It was presumably these same routes that communities of settlers from the continent had been using for over 100 years, bringing with them their burial rites and knowledge of ceramics. It appears that there were political links between the Atrebates in Britain and in Gaul, and between tribal members in Britain and the Suessiones in Gaul, through which military reinforcements could have been provided. It is also likely that reports from traders had led Caesar to expect rich plunder and an abundance of captives to serve or be sold as slaves. The publicity would be useful too in the furtherance of his political career.

Caesar's flagship reached the British coast near Dover at about 9 a.m. The British Celts were waiting for him. Already, he could see 'ranks of armed men lined up along the cliff tops. Such was the nature of the terrain, so steep the cliff face down to the sea, that missiles could be hurled from the heights on to the shore' (Caesar, *Gallic Wars* IV. 23). When the rest of the convoy caught up with him at about 3 p.m., he ordered it to follow him to a point 6½ miles (10km) to the north, where he beached the transports as near to the shore as their draught would allow. All the time, the British Celts shadowed his movements from the coast, sending their cavalry and chariots on ahead to stop the Romans disembarking.

They almost succeeded. While the troops held back, unwilling to jump into the surf and wade to the shore in full kit, the Celts hurled javelins from the beach or actually drove their horses into the sea against the invaders. Caesar, whose first amphibious engagement this was, ordered some of his warships to withdraw, and then row like mad in a circle to attack the Celts from the flank with artillery, arrows, and slingshot. Still the legionaries were reluctant to take the plunge. Then the standard-bearer of the Tenth, giving a hasty prayer for luck, leaped into the sea and began to wade towards the enemy, holding the eagle-emblem aloft. The men followed, desperate to avoid the disgrace of losing it.

On the beach, there was chaos, with the Romans, as they straggled ashore, unable to form up in their normal units, and being picked off one by one. Without his cavalry, Caesar manned his ships' longboats and his reconnaissance vessels with soldiers and used them as a support force, until his legionaries were able to form up and mount a charge. The Celts were routed, and required to provide hostages.

It was not until four days later that the cavalry transports were able to sail, and they immediately ran into a gale from the east. Some were blown back to Gaul, others were forced off course to westward, but managed to cast anchor, only to start taking water as the waves crashed over the gunwales. They stood out to sea again and, after a night of foul weather, returned to the continent.

Worse followed. Unknown to the Roman camp, the gale coincided with the highest tide of the month. This caused havoc to the warships drawn up on the beach, while the storm severely damaged the transports riding out at anchor, several of which broke up.

With food supplies getting low, Caesar sent out the Seventh Legion to cut corn. The Celts swooped on the men from the woods in which they had hidden overnight, and would have overcome them had not Caesar, alerted by the dust rising, come to the rescue. Buoyed up by the possibility of success against a hungry and debilitated force, the Celts called up reinforcements and attacked the Roman camp. The legions, able to form up in their usual fashion, beat them off, but without cavalry Caesar was unable to follow up his initial success.

With winter approaching, he crammed his men into the vessels that had been salvaged from the storm and tide, and sailed back to Gaul. Though he had doubled the number of hostages required, and ordered them to report to him on the continent, many never turned up. It had been an inglorious campaign, but Caesar had gained his personal glory. The senate decreed a public celebration of 20 days: 'For seeing that the formerly unknown had become certain and the previously unheard-of accessible, they regarded the hope for the future inspired by these facts as already realized and exulted over their expected acquisitions as if they were already within their grasp' (Cassius Dio, tr. Earnest Cary, *Roman History* XXXIX. 53. 2). What better incentive could Caesar have had to return the following year? For all that, he needed to rethink his aspirations with regard to loot. As Cicero pointed out in a letter to his friend Atticus, there did not seem to be the slightest trace of silver in Britain, and no booty except low-value slaves, who did not have the musical or secretarial skills to fetch high prices. And if Caesar really did, as Suetonius (c.AD 70–c.140) suggests, sail in hope of finding pearls, on which he was something of an authority, he must have been deeply disappointed, as British pearls were of poor quality.

Before he left Gaul for his winter break in his Italian province, as was his custom, he ordered a new fleet of 28 warships and 600 transports, the latter of shallower draught but broader than before, and equipped with oars as well as a sail. The final fleet numbered over 800 and included private vessels owned or hired by merchants expecting pickings from the campaign. Caesar had with him five legions and 2,000 auxiliary cavalry. His deputy, Titus Labienus (d. 45 BC), was left behind with three legions and 2,000 cavalry to maintain order in Gaul and keep the corn supplies moving across to Britain. With Caesar's private entourage were a number of high-ranking Gallic hostages; he felt that there might be less trouble in Gaul if he had them with him. These did not include Dumnorix, chief of the Aedui, who had pleaded, among other excuses, that he was a bad sailor. Caesar refused his request, but Dumnorix escaped. Though his army was already beginning to embark after being delayed by a north-west wind for 25 days, Caesar cancelled the sailing and sent a troop of cavalry after Dumnorix, who was hunted down and killed.

The invasion fleet finally sailed at about 9 p.m. on 6 July 54 BC. At about 1 a.m. the south-west breeze dropped, and the ships were carried on the tide up-channel towards the North Sea. At sunrise Caesar saw the coast rapidly receding on the port quarter. Taking advantage of the turning of the tide, he ordered the troops to take to the oars and row the transports to a suitable landing place. There followed an extraordinary boat race, in which the amateur oarsmen in the heavily-laden transports kept pace with the professionals in the warships – naval rowers were not slaves, but freeborn provincials.

The landing, on the beaches near Deal at about 11.30 a.m., was unopposed, the Celts having taken one look at the armada and withdrawn. Caesar left his ships riding at anchor off shore, guarded by a garrison of ten cohorts (about 5,000 men) and 300 cavalry, and at about 1 a.m. set off in pursuit – surprise was one of his tactical trade marks. After a night march of 11 miles (18km), he caught up with the opposition on the river Stour near Bigbury. Caesar forced the Celts to retire to a hilltop fortified position, which he took. He then rested his troops overnight, and sent them off the following morning in three detachments to pursue the fugitives. They had actually made contact with the slowest of these, when dispatch riders arrived from Caesar with orders to return immediately. Disaster had struck the fleet again.

In a storm the previous night cables had snapped and anchors dragged, throwing many of the ships up onto the beach; others cannoned into each other, breaking bows and smashing hulls. Forty were a total loss; the rest might conceivably be repaired. Caesar withdrew all the carpenters from the legions and set them to work. Others were recruited from the continent, and orders were sent to Labienus to set his legions to building as many new ships as possible. Ten days later, all the ships had been hauled up on the beach, within an extension to the palisades and trenched defences of the main camp, and the work of patching them up was under way. Then Caesar set out again after the Celts.

The meteorological intervention had enabled the Celts of south-east Britain to unite under a single leader of considerable imagination and strategic ability, Cassivellaunus, whose tribe was based to the north of the river Thames. The subsequent campaign lasted for two months. In the course of it Caesar marched his men from Deal to the Thames at Brentford, possibly for part of the way following the old track along the ridge of the North Downs, and then to Wheathampstead, and back, a round trip of about 300 miles (480km). For most of the time they were harried by contingents of cavalry and two-horse chariots, built to a Celtic design, with spoked wheels fitted with a one-piece resilient iron rim, and some sort of suspension. These would swoop when least expected, and then retire again. At some point during the early part of the march, Caesar deployed three of his legions, with supporting cavalry, against a considerable Celtic force, and routed it. When he reached the Thames, however, there, manoeuvring on the flat land on the opposite side of the river, were several thousand chariots. Cassivellaunus was waiting for him, and somehow he had got his chariots across the ford. He had also fortified the bank above and below the water-line with sharpened stakes projecting outwards.

According to Caesar's own account, the water at that point must have been 4ft 6in (1.4m) deep. He sent the cavalry across first, followed by the legions, with only their heads above water. Such was the efficiency of their deployment, and the force of their attack, that the Celts melted away. Caesar headed for Wheathampstead, the centre of operations of Cassivellaunus, who used so effectively the 4,000 chariots he had retained that Caesar was unable to detach his cavalry from the column for fear of it being cut off. Cassivellaunus stalked Caesar's movements, moving people and cattle into the shelter of the woods ahead of the Roman line of march. Caesar retaliated by burning the crops on the way.

That Caesar won the final showdown was largely due to a fifth columnist, Mandubracius of the Trinovantes, whose father, chief of the tribe, had been killed by Cassivellaunus. Mandubracius offered the services of his tribe in searching out Cassivellaunus and in providing corn for the legions in return for protection and for recognition by Rome. Smaller tribes in the area followed suit. Cassivellaunus made a last ditch attempt to prevent Caesar's return to Gaul by encouraging the tribes in Kent to make an assault on the Roman naval base. This failed when the Roman garrison surged out from behind the defences and put the Celts to flight. Wheathampstead capitulated to a two-pronged attack, and Cassivellaunus sued for peace. Caesar's negotiator was Commius, chief of the Atrebates in Gaul, who also claimed to rule the Atrebates in Britain.

Caesar's relief must have been considerable, because what he ingenu-
ously refers to as 'unexpected disturbances' (*Gallic Wars* V. 22) called for his
immediate attention in Gaul. He requisitioned numerous hostages and fixed
an annual tribute from Britain to Rome, though there is no evidence that
it was ever paid. The cross-channel withdrawal was once again hazardous.
Most of the transports he had sent back empty and the new ships built for
him by Labienus never made it to Britain because of the weather. Having
waited for them for several days, Caesar packed his troops, his hostages, and
his prisoners-of-war into his refurbished fleet, and got across to Gaul just
before the autumnal equinox, which occurred about 23 September.

It would be 97 years before the legions were seen in Britain again.
On the face of it, Caesar had achieved little. He had, however, proved
that Britain could be invaded, and he was instrumental in the establishment of links with tribes in Britain friendly to, or frightened of, Rome.
Whatever his motives, without his initiative Britain would probably
never have become part of the Roman empire.

The archaeological evidence for the beginning of the Romanisation
of Britain is in the form of coins. At the end of the first century BC
three chiefs, Tincommius, Eppillus, and Verica, probably all descended
from Commius, ruled over parts of south-east Britain. At some point,
the design of their coins ceased to follow the Celtic style and became
so like that of Rome that they may have been struck from dies engraved
by Romans. The same was the case north of the Thames, where
Cunobelin (Shakespeare's Cymbeline) united the territories of the
powerful Trinovantes and Catuvellauni under his rule, making
Camulodunum (Colchester) his capital.

From 49 BC Caesar ruled the Roman empire constitutionally and
energetically as dictator – the Latin means 'commander', someone who
gives orders. He pushed through the senate many beneficial measures,
but he tried to make too many changes too quickly. The 13 years that
followed his assassination in 44 BC by a group of disaffected officials,
former soldiers, and members of the senate, who feared a return to a
monarchy, were the most savage and bloody in the history of Rome.
With the defeat and suicide of Mark Antony (83–30 BC) and his para-
mour Cleopatra (Cleopatra VII, 68–30 BC), a former mistress of Caesar,
the 31-year-old Octavian, whom Caesar had nominated as his principal
heir, was the undisputed controller of the Roman world. In 27 BC he
effectively became emperor, renaming himself Augustus and assuming

5 Principal Celtic tribes of Britain

the title of *princeps* ('first' or 'chief'). A careful, contemplative person, and something of a hypochondriac, he considered a full invasion of Britain, which would have given him military glory to match that of the flamboyant Antony. The time, however, never seemed right, especially after AD 9, when Quinctilius Varus, at the head of a Roman army, was ambushed in a wooded mountain pass in Germania. Three legions were destroyed, Germania was lost to Rome, and Augustus was traumatised. He died in AD 14, having expressly stated that his successors should not attempt to extend the boundaries of the empire in any direction.

That his instructions were ultimately ignored was due to a combination of circumstances. Both Suetonius and Cassius Dio record the story of how the mad Caligula prepared an invasion of Britain, embarked in a warship, then changed his mind, and ordered the legions instead to gather sea shells, which he took back to Rome as the spoils of victory. This exploit, however, reminded the authorities of Caesar's unfinished British business. There was also a risk that hostile elements, only a few sea miles beyond the northern boundary of the empire, could easily upset the balance of power. Further, if, as has been suggested, some of the friendly tribes were also client kingdoms of Rome, it made better tactical sense to subdue the whole country than to keep having to come to the aid of individual groupings, as had happened in Gaul during Caesar's campaigns. The prevailing situation had also left the Roman garrison on the Rhine dangerously over strength in the event of dissatisfaction among the troops there. For Caligula had raised two new legions for his invasion, which had then been allocated to the Rhine station.

Caligula was assassinated in AD 41, and his 50-year-old uncle Claudius found himself emperor. In an age of serial removals of heirs to the imperial throne, he had survived so long probably because his disabilities, chronic ill health, stammer, and general air of mental deficiency (which may have been deliberately assumed), ensured that people left him alone. Though he had no experience of administration, he became a sound and constructive ruler, as also did Elizabeth I, Victoria, George VI, and Elizabeth II. Claudius was a scholar and historian, perfectly capable of imbibing and learning from the experiences of the past. His choice of women was disastrous, but then so has been that of other prominent public figures. He was dominated by his personal staff of freedmen, many of whom enriched themselves in the process, but he may have preferred that to being dominated by corrupt officials and members of the senate.

Cunobelin died between AD 40 and 42, leaving his territorial interests to his sons, Togodumnus, the elder, and Caratacus. While Togodumnus was consolidating his affairs north of the Thames, Caratacus, probably in an attempt to increase his influence, was causing disturbances among the pro-Roman tribes in Kent and Sussex. He also expelled Verica, who had assumed the leadership of the British Atrebates. Verica travelled to Rome, and complained to Claudius of his treatment. Claudius now had an excuse to invade Britain, and at the same time to reduce the risk of potential trouble from legions on the Rhine frontier. He also saw the advantage of adding military prowess to his list of personal accomplishments.

Four legions, three of them from the Rhine frontier, and as many auxiliary troops, probably 40,000 men in all, were assembled at the coast, with 15,000 animals, including pack horses and mules. Claudius had appointed Aulus Plautius, a distant cousin of his first wife, as commander of the invasion force, with instructions to ask for his help if he got into any difficulties. It is likely that Plautius's orders were to call on the emperor to preside over, and take the credit for, the final victory.

It has been suggested that the invasion fleet numbered nearly 1,000 vessels in all. Embarking the troops and animals, wherever precisely this took place, and maintaining some kind of formation during the night crossing, were complicated enough. The disembarkation of such a force would have been a logistical nightmare. It may be that there were three separate landing places. Opinion, based on the latest archaeological evidence, is divided as to whether the fleet made for Richborough in Kent, which can be seen from the French coast, or Fishbourne, on the Solent, which would have involved a longer passage.

The landing, in late June or early July AD 43, was unopposed. Plautius subsequently defeated the forces of both Togodumnus and Caratacus, on each occasion by tactical use of Celtic auxiliaries from the Batavian settlements on the Rhine estuary, who were trained to swim across rivers in full armour. Three weeks later, Plautius was in a position to launch an attack on the crucial fortress-city of Camulodunum, effectively the British capital. Instead, as arranged, he sent a dispatch to Claudius requesting the emperor's personal assistance.

Claudius had been waiting for the call, for which extensive preparations had already been made. These, according to Cassius Dio, included the enlistment of an imperial escort of elephants. Elephants were much in demand as emblems of authority – after the public feast celebrating his quadruple triumph in 46 BC, Caesar was escorted home by elephants carrying torches. Though they had a use in war for terrorising the opposition, and their smell caused horses to panic, this was not a Roman way of fighting a battle. And Claudius, as a historian, would know that at the final battle of the civil war between Caesar and the followers of Pompey, at Thapsus in Africa in 46 BC, the elephants loaned to the Pompeians by the king of Numidia ran amok and trampled to death troops of their own side.

However the elephants got to Britain, or whether they were already there, Claudius himself set off by barge to Ostia, the port of Rome at the mouth of the Tiber. His personal entourage included several senatorial advisers, the commander of the praetorian guard (the emperor's personal protection force), and Claudius's two sons-in-law, Gnaeus Pompeius Magnus, whose mother was descended from Pompey the 'Great', and Lucius Junius Silanus. Pompeius had married Antonia, daughter of Claudius's second wife, Aelia Paetina; Silanus, then only 16, was betrothed to the infant Octavia (AD 39–62), daughter of Claudius's third wife, the notorious Messalina, who was executed in AD 48. From Ostia, the party sailed along the coast to Massilia (Marseilles), twice almost being shipwrecked. Their passage through Gaul to their port of embarkation was partly by land and partly by river.

The whole journey would have taken at least a month. Suetonius tells us that the future emperor Vespasian (AD 9–79), while in Britain at the beginning of the rule of Claudius, fought 30 battles, defeated two hostile tribes, and took more than 20 towns, as well as the whole of the Isle of Wight. According to Tacitus, Vespasian was appointed by Claudius to command the Second Legion in Britain, where he fought with distinction. If we allow that one of the two tribes was the Durotriges, that by towns is meant hill-forts, and that part anyway of the fleet was standing by at Fishbourne, then it is perfectly feasible that this campaign was conducted while the army waited for the arrival of the emperor. The archaeological evidence, however, is at best equivocal.

Claudius spent just 16 days in Britain. Camulodunum was duly occupied, and other pseudo-military exploits organised for his gratification. Pompeius and Silanus were sent ahead to Rome to deliver the good news. The senate immediately bestowed on Claudius, and also on his two-year-old son Tiberius (AD 41–55), the title of Britannicus, and

granted the emperor a triumph. Claudius spent several months savour-
ing his success on an imperial progress back to Rome and glory.

A triumphal arch was erected in the city in the name of the senate
and people of Rome, with an inscription, carved in AD 52, to the effect
that Claudius received the submission of 11 kings of the Britons. These
would no doubt have included the tribes who were already pro-
Roman, the Atrebates, Catuvellauni, Dobunni, and Regni. The Iceni
and Brigantes (under their queen, Cartimandua) also probably fell into
this category. The Cantiaci and the Durotriges must have been among
those subdued, though Caratacus himself survived to fight again, as
leader of the Ordovices and Silures in Wales.

Plautius may have summoned some if not all of these 'kings' or their
representatives personally to bow before the emperor. Other evidence suggests that the submission was a more gradual process. There is on the face
of it an extraordinary statement in the historian Eutropius (*fl. c.* AD 370):
'[Claudius] also added to the Roman empire certain islands in the sea
beyond Britain called the Orkneys' (VII. 13). This assertion also occurs in
the history of the world by the fifth-century ecclesiastic Orosius. That the
Orcades were being overrun by immigrants forced to seek new homelands
by an influx of Celts from the south is possible. This being so, it is perfectly feasible that they should act as other Celtic tribes had done in Gaul and
Britain, and seek Rome's protection against their unruly neighbours. At
some point, then, in the ensuing nine years, an Orcadian diplomatic mission travelled by sea, maybe all the way along the east coast of Britain, to
be received in the emperor's name at Camulodunum, legionary fortress
and Claudius's provincial capital. There would seem to be archaeological
evidence to support this. Fragments of pottery discovered in a broch settlement in Orkney are from a Roman amphora of a design which was not
manufactured after AD 60. No other examples of this type have been
found in Britain nearer than Essex, in which is the town of Colchester
(Camulodunum).

The provincial acquisition that Claudius now left Plautius and his
legions to administer was largely uncharted territory, with a great diver-
sity of types of terrain, inhabited by tribes and tribal groupings some of
whom were inimical to each other as well as to Rome. Plautius concentrated his efforts east of a line that might be drawn between the
rivers Humber and Severn. Legionary fortresses, forts, and signal stations
had to be built, linked by roads which often followed existing trackways.

Trade followed the army, to supply its needs and also to pick up local business. Celts, who previously had built only in wood, found themselves introduced to the craft of stonemasonry, and to the use of such indigenous resources as Bath stone and Purbeck marble. Deposits of clay were in demand for making tiles for roofing and for central heating systems. Extensive searches were conducted for minerals, especially gold and silver, and the existing iron-fields were extended and new ones exploited. Gold deposits were largely inaccessible, some being in Scotland, but once Wales was subdued, a mine was dug and worked in Carmarthenshire. Cicero was both right and wrong about the silver. It was obtainable as a by-product of lead ore, but the content was negligible, though the lead proved invaluable for water tanks and pipes.

Everything was under military control, exercised where applicable through the principle of client kingdoms, under leaders indebted or subservient to Rome. Such were Cogidubnus, king of the Regni, who became so Romanised as to call himself Tiberius Claudius Cogidubnus, Prasutagus of the Iceni, and Cartimandua, the queen who ruled a federation of Brigantine tribes which effectively created a temporary buffer zone between the Roman interests in the south-east and the northern Celtic tribes. West of the fortified zone which represented the boundary of Roman influence lay the mountainous terrain of Wales, where the Ordovices and Silures had accepted the leadership of Caratacus. Beyond them, on the sacred island of Anglesey, the druids weaved their spells and plotted means of ridding Britain of the Romans, on which their survival depended. For in Gaul they had been banned from practising their rites by Augustus's successor, his stepson Tiberius (42 BC–AD 37), and also by Claudius. It was not, however, just the rites themselves which were objectionable; it was also the fact that the druids exercised considerable political clout which transcended tribal divisions.

Predictably, the first sign of trouble was from Wales, timed for the winter of AD 47/48, when Plautius had left after his stint as governor and his replacement, Ostorius Scapula, had not yet reached Britain. On his arrival, Scapula hastily mustered his troops, who were not used to operating in winter, let alone a British winter, and forced the Celts to retire temporarily to their side of the river Severn. Then, in an effort to neutralise the influence the druids were capable of exercising over ostensibly pro-Roman tribes, he attempted to disarm not only all members of those tribes of whom he had reason to feel suspicious, but also all subjects of the client kingdoms. Some of the Iceni caused a rebellion, which had to be put down.

Caratacus now rallied the Celts of Wales, and Scapula made his second political gaffe. In order to release a legion for the Welsh front, and still protect his interests to his rear, he withdrew the Twentieth Legion from Camulodunum, which he made instead into a permanent colony for veteran soldiers. The behaviour of these, and the cool and brutal manner in which they appropriated land belonging to the locals, incensed the Trinovantes, in whose territory the colony was.

Caratacus was defeated and took refuge with the Brigantes, but was handed over to the Romans by Cartimandua, and triumphantly taken to Rome. There, Claudius, having accepted the credit for his capture, pardoned Caratacus and his family, who lived out their lives in Rome. This was in direct contrast to the treatment meted out by Julius Caesar to Vercingetorix, another Celtic military commander of talent and nobility. After parading Vercingetorix in chains at his triumph in 46 BC, Caesar had him strangled!

The Welsh problem did not go away. Scapula died of stress in AD 51. Before his successor, Didius Gallus, arrived, the Silures had taken on and defeated a legion. Didius succeeded in restoring some sort of order, only to be faced with sorting out a delicate situation when the Brigantes rebelled against Cartimandua, their own (pro-Roman) queen, in the course of a long-running dispute between her and her husband.

Claudius died in AD 54, poisoned by his fourth wife, and was succeeded by her son Nero, now aged 16. Nero's official advisers counselled him to abandon Britain. He considered the idea, but turned it down as reflecting badly on the glory of his stepfather. Didius carried on until AD 57, managing, in the words of Tacitus, to 'keep things just under control' (*The Annals* XIV. 29). His successor, Quintus Veranius, died after a year in office, having naively informed Nero in his will that given another two years he could have finished the job!

Veranius was replaced by Suetonius Paulinus, who 16 years earlier had successfully suppressed a revolt in the newly acquired province of Mauretania; he also had experience of mountain warfare. His tactics were to obliterate the druidical centre on the island of Anglesey. His men torched sanctuaries and destroyed the sacred groves. While this was going on, Paulinus got the news of serious trouble among the Iceni. He left a garrison on Anglesey, without ever discovering whether or not he had simply driven the druids underground.

The Romans had come to Britain as a military not a spiritual force, such as was the spread of Christianity in pagan lands. The extinction of the druids was seen as a matter primarily of political expediency. It was successful in that the term 'druid' was not used again in Britain until much later. The influence of the druids, however, must have survived in some form in both Britain and Gaul, and the druids reappear in Irish and British accounts as *magi*.

The trouble in Britain, which flared up into a full-scale rebellion, had its origins in Roman insensitivity. Prasutagus had died. Instead of leaving everything to the emperor, as the Romans thought was customary for a client king, he appointed Nero his heir jointly with his two daughters, no doubt hoping in this way that his kingdom would be preserved. The Roman garrison thought otherwise. Prasutagus's possessions were ransacked, his widow Boudica was stripped and flogged, and her daughters were raped. Hereditary lands of the chiefs of the tribe were confiscated in the emperor's name. In AD 60, the Iceni, under Boudica, went on the rampage, joined by the Trinovantes, smarting not only from the behaviour of the colonists but from a decision of the senate to build in Camulodunum a great temple to the glory of the deified Claudius, towards which local chiefs were required to contribute. There is no doubt, too, that the druids, from their island fastness, had fomented the initial unrest.

Camulodunum was overrun and its garrison, and their households, slaughtered. A scratch force mustered by Petillius Cerialis, commander of the Ninth Legion, was ambushed and destroyed, though he himself escaped. London and Verulamium (St Albans) were sacked. Graves were desecrated. Unspeakable atrocities were perpetrated on women of distinction under the guise of religious observance. Paulinus, however, bided his time, and chose his ground carefully. The site has tentatively been identified as Mancetter, near Atherstone, Warwickshire, on the main military route to the north-west later known as Watling Street. The Roman lines were protected at the rear by woodlands, with a narrow defile to the front, through which the Celtic forces would have to advance in order to reach their enemy. The battle, between a desperate but overexcited and unruly horde of maybe 100,000 Celts and about 12,000 trained and disciplined legionaries and auxiliaries, was watched by a vast audience of Celtic camp followers, including women and children, sitting on wagons drawn up in a semicircle behind and to the left of Boudica's army. The result, though hard fought, was a massacre, not only of the Celtic fighting men, but also of the spectators, who could not get out of the way of the headlong retreat. Boudica is said to have poisoned herself.

Paulinus followed up his victory with a policy of oppression against tribes who had contributed to the revolt, which in turn led to conditions of famine. There ensued a difference of opinion between Paulinus and Julius Classicianus, a Romanised Gaul, who arrived as the new provincial finance administrator and deputy governor. Classicianus was of the opinion that violence would continue as long as Paulinus remained in his post as governor. The emperor set up an enquiry, conducted by an imperial freedman, which exonerated Paulinus. Shortly afterwards, however, Nero made the inadvertent loss of a few ships and their crews an excuse to recall him. The governorships of Petronius Turpilianus (AD 61–63) and Trebellius Maximus (AD 63–69) were unremarkable and went largely unnoticed, except insofar as there was no uprising of the tribes during the sequence of events which traumatised the empire in AD 68/69.

Nero's excesses finally became too much for the senate, which in AD 68 had declared him a public enemy and sentenced him to death by flogging. Nero thought about flight, but instead committed suicide. Within a year, three emperors had come and gone, Galba (hacked to death by the imperial guard), Otho (suicide), and Vitellius (killed by the mob), and a fourth had been acclaimed. This was Titus Flavius Sabinus Vespasianus (Vespasian), a 60-year-old professional soldier, who was away in Judaea reducing the Jewish people to submission after a revolt had flared up in AD 66. He left his son Titus (AD 40–81) to conduct the siege of Jerusalem itself, and arrived back in Rome in October AD 70.

Vitellius had just had time to appoint Vettius Bolanus to succeed Trebellius. Bolanus, by all accounts, was an easy-going man, who may not have had the diplomatic skills or military resources to deal properly with the next crisis. Cartimandua, finally tiring either of her violent husband Venutius or else simply of his anti-Roman attitude, divorced him and married his armour-bearer, Vellocatus. Fighting between two factions was intensified by an incursion into the tribal lands of the Brigantes by an outside force of pro-Venutius agitators. Bolanus sent some cohorts of auxiliaries, who whisked Cartimandua away to safety, but succeeded in doing little else. The Brigantes were in a state of revolt, and from now on Roman attention was permanently directed towards the north of the province. Opinions hotly vary as to which governor first crossed the line between the Clyde and Forth estuaries. The poet Statius (c. AD 45–96), in a eulogy of Bolanus addressed to the governor's son, observes, 'What if the land tamed by your illustrious father were to receive you. . . how much glory shall attend Caledonian fields of battle' (*Silvae* V. ii. 140–2). This may be poetic licence, or it may refer to the pursuit of the Brigantian Venutius into southern Scotland.

Much more enigmatic is the statement about Britain by Pliny the Elder (AD 23–79) in his encyclopaedic work, *Natural History*, written in AD 77: 'Nearly thirty years ago, its exploration was carried out by the armed forces of Rome to a point beyond the neighbourhood of the Caledonian Forest' (tr. H. Rackham, IV. 102). Pliny was a workaholic polymath with an intense thirst for knowledge; when he was not himself reading, he was being read to. He supplemented his reading with his own scientific observations, dying of asphyxiation while recording the phenomena caused by the eruption of Vesuvius. The Caledonian Forest is no metaphor for some part of northernmost Britain. The second-century AD geographer Ptolemy places it very precisely to the west of the territory of the Caledonians, which according to him stretched effectively from Loch Fyne to the Moray Firth. 'Nearly thirty years ago' would take us to the governorship of Ostorius Scapula, who was, as we have seen, totally preoccupied with the problem of the Welsh. In any case, Claudius, who had already had his glory, would have been unlikely to have given Scapula permission to campaign so far north.

Another contender is Bolanus's successor, Petillius Cerialis, he who lost part of his legion in the uprising of Boudica. He had redeemed himself, however, in AD 70 by suppressing a Celtic revolt in the lower reaches of the Rhine. This had been instigated by the Batavi, who had become aggrieved at the overenthusiastic recruiting methods of the Roman military. Petillius was the first of three governors of Britain appointed by Vespasian. He arrived in AD 71, and from the start was pretty much preoccupied with the problem of the Brigantes. It required numerous minor but hard-fought battles before the tribe, once a compliant client-kingdom, became instead another potentially dangerous annex to the growing province of Britain.

Petillius is generally supposed to have founded the legionary fortress at York, in the heart of the territory of the Brigantes. To the end of his campaign is attributed the line of marching camps running from Catterick roughly north-west: Bowes Moor, Rey Cross, Warcop, Crackenthorpe, Kirkby Thore, Penrith, Plumpton Head, Barrock Fell, Golden Fleece, to Carlisle, where archaeological evidence suggests that there could have been a fort established as early as AD 72 or 73. There is growing archaeological evidence too that from Carlisle Petillius ventured into southern Scotland. Certainly, traces of temporary structures which could be linked to his period as governor have been found at Burnswark, Dalswinton, and even as far north as Bankhead and Loudoun Hill, while there is a suggestion of more permanent occupation at Milton (Tassiesholm).

Petillius was recalled to Rome in late AD 73 or early 74. In AD 70 he had served as *consul suffectus*, 'substitute' or 'deputy' consul. With one of the two consulships being occupied by the emperor and, in the case of Vespasian, the other by his elder son Titus, there were no longer enough ex-consuls available for consular posts, such as governorships of major provinces. To rectify this, one or both consuls for the year would resign halfway through their term of office in favour of a substitute. Petillius was appointed by Vespasian to be *consul suffectus* for a second time, in AD 74.

Petillius's replacement as governor was Sextus Julius Frontinus (*c.*AD 40–103), a career soldier with an interest in engineering – he later wrote a treatise on aqueducts which reveals him as an energetic and punctilious reformer. He directed his methodical approach to the consolidation of the southern region of the province. This involved subduing the troublesome Silures, and beginning the construction of legionary fortresses at Caerleon and Chester. He also established coastal forts at Neath, Loughor, and Carmarthen, and probably the base at Cardiff. He was recalled in AD 77 or 78, having begun a campaign to occupy the territory of the Ordovices.

Gnaeus Julius Agricola (AD 40–93) was chosen by Vespasian to succeed Frontinus as governor of Britain. He had served twice in Britain before, and had spent the years AD 74–77 sharpening his administrative skills in the plum job of governor of Aquitania, an extensive province so peaceful that it had no permanent legionary garrison. A term as *consul suffectus* followed in 77. He was 37, and, thanks to a piece of family legerdemain, he has become probably the best known Roman in Britain after Julius Caesar.

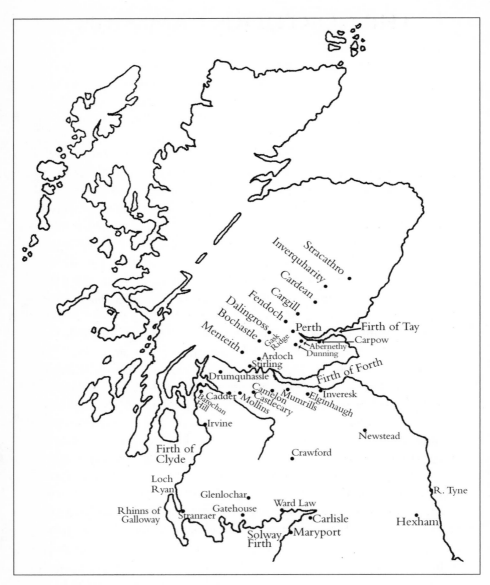

Stracathro

Inverquharity

Cardean

Cargill

Fendoch

Dalingross

Bochastle

Menteith

Gask Ridge

Perth

Firth of Tay

Carpow

Abernethy

Dunning

Ardoch

Stirling

Firth of Forth

Drumquhassle

Camelon

Mumrills

Elginhaugh

Inveresk

Cadder

Castlecary

Bar Hill

Mollins

Barochan Hill

Irvine

Newstead

Firth of Clyde

Crawford

Loch Ryan

Glenlochar

Ward Law

R. Tyne

Rhinns of Galloway

Stranraer

Gatehouse

Carlisle

Hexham

Maryport

Solway Firth

6 Scotland, first century AD, with places mentioned in chapter 4

4

THE NORTHERN CAMPAIGN

Agricola was born on 13 June AD 40, in the Mediterranean coastal town and naval station of Forum Julii, in Transalpine Gaul, the province from which Caesar launched his Gallic campaign in 58 BC. Both Agricola's grandfathers had been provincial administrators of equestrian rank. His father, Julius Graecinus, was a senator who had served as praetor, the rank below consul. He was much favoured by Tiberius, but fell foul of Caligula, who apparently had him executed, shortly after Agricola's birth, for refusing to act as prosecutor in a case against one of the emperor's personal *bêtes noires*. Agricola was brought up by his mother, Julia Procilla, of distinguished Romanised Celtic descent. She is likely to have been Graecinus's second wife, young, and so loyal to his memory that she chose not to marry again.

It was probably in the interests of Agricola's education that his mother moved to Massilia (Marseilles), the academic centre of excellence for Roman Gaul, where he would have received a solid grounding in Greek literature and thought, and in public speaking. The only career opportunities available to a young man of his class and upbringing were the army, the law, or politics. He chose to follow his father into politics, and to rise as high as he could on the *cursus honorum*, the 'ladder of honour', which at various stages could also involve military service. As a first step he served in Britain under Suetonius Paulinus as the senior of six military tribunes (equivalent to staff officer) in a legion, during the Boudican rebellion. He was quaestor in AD 64 (serving in an administrative post in Asia), tribune of the people in 66, and praetor in 68, in which capacity Galba commissioned him to investigate malpractices with regard to gifts donated to temples. In the meantime he had married, probably in AD 62, Domitia Decidiana, like himself of an illustrious family from Transalpine Gaul. They had a son, who died in infancy, and in AD 64 or 65 a daughter, Julia, who survived.

The year AD 69 was Agricola's watershed. During the brief rule of Otho from January to April, some navy louts went on the rampage in the vicinity of Nice, looting and murdering. Among the dead was Agricola's mother, on her country estate. It would appear that while Agricola was attending to her affairs he learned that Vespasian was proposing to challenge Vitellius for the imperial throne, and immediately pledged his support. It was a dangerous but fateful decision. Vespasian was proclaimed by the army in Egypt as rival to Vitellius on 1 July, 16 days before Vitellius arrived in Rome as emperor. He succeeded Vitellius on 21 December, but did not reach Rome until October of the following year. In the meantime his right-hand man, Licinius Mucianus, had despatched Agricola to Britain to assume command, under Vettius Bolanus, Vitellius's man, of the difficult Twentieth Legion, whose loyalty to Vespasian was suspect.

Petillius Cerialis arrived in Britain in AD 71. His full name was Quintus Petillius Cerialis Caesius Rufus. He was, according to Tacitus, 'closely related by marriage to Vespasian' (*Histories* 3. 59), from which it has been understood that he was Vespasian's brother-in-law or son-in-law. Under his overall leadership, there was much more military action, in which the Twentieth operated on the north-western front of the provincial territory. Agricola's reward, on his recall to Rome in AD 74, was to be elevated to the nobility, and made governor of Aquitania. In AD 77 he gave his daughter Julia, just into her teens, in marriage to Cornelius Tacitus, a 20-year-old high-flyer, also from Transalpine Gaul.

After serving as *consul suffectus*, Agricola was sent back by Vespasian to Britain, this time as governor, with four legions under his command. The year was either AD 77 or 78; for the purposes of this book, I have based my account on the later date. That we know more about Agricola, and about his seven-year term of office, than any other governor of Britain is entirely due to Tacitus, whose first book, published in AD 98, was a posthumous life of his father-in-law, *De Vita Agricola* (On the Life of Agricola), usually known as the *Agricola*. With it, however, comes a health warning. It is the sole historical source of information about Agricola's Scottish campaigns, and it first came to light in Germany in the fifteenth century. Even today, only four manuscripts are known, one of them being a copy of one of the others, which are themselves imperfect texts. Further, Tacitus is sometimes difficult to translate with any certainty, or even to interpret.

What then is the *Agricola*? By modern standards it is a short work, being not much more than 7,000 words. Though Tacitus states that his aim is to honour his father-in-law, the book is still far too long to be regarded simply as a funeral oration. Nor would one expect, in a work whose sole purpose was to glorify its subject, to have 20 per cent of its extent devoted to a geographical and ethnological outline of Britain and a historical sketch of its early conquest.

The *Agricola* is a biography, of which there was already a Roman tradition, following Greek models. Tacitus is observing the literary conventions of the time in his explanatory and apologetic preface and complementary epilogue. The book has political overtones in that the character of Agricola is compared with that of the tyrannical Domitian, younger brother and successor of the glamorous Titus, and the third and last of the Flavian dynasty of emperors. To make the distinction crystal clear Tacitus represents Agricola as having the conventional qualities that are attributed to brilliant generals and eminent administrators, which he may not fully have deserved. The account also reflects Tacitus's personal views on the integration of other cultures into the Roman ethos. The ancient historians were primarily, however, concerned with telling a story, and it is as a story that his book was expected to be judged. In spite of the fact that its author is paying homage to an admired father-in-law, when the *Agricola* is stripped of its geographical vagueness, its generalisations, and its well-meant exaggerations, there is no reason to ignore it as a unique outline of historical events and of one man's contribution to them.

Agricola's brief from Vespasian would have been to consolidate the Roman conquests in Britain, Romanise for their own benefit, and unify and civilise (which meant also urbanise) the conquered, and extend the frontiers of the empire. At his disposal were the legions Second Augusta (based at Caerleon), Ninth Hispana (York), Twentieth Valeria Victrix (Agricola's former command, based at Wroxeter), and Second Adiutrix (Chester), which had replaced the Fourteenth Gemina in AD 71. The naval fleet, *classis Britannica*, was standing by at Boulogne, and would be employed by Agricola on his Scottish campaigns. Straddling the territory south of Carlisle there were already over 100 fortresses, forts, and fortlets guarding major and minor routes, overlooking potential trouble spots, protecting friendly tribes from their neighbours, or serving as bases for the local military government.

During what appears to have been the inevitable interregnum between one governor being recalled and the next taking office, the Ordovices had taken the opportunity of ambushing and wiping out a cavalry regiment operating in the Welsh mountains. It was now so late in the season that the regular troops had retired to their winter quarters. Agricola mustered a scratch force of auxiliaries and men on detachment duties, attacked the main base of the Ordovices up hill, and destroyed it. He then completed the conquest of Wales by using his amphibious Batavian units to swim across the Menai Strait, probably to the southern tip of the island, and take Anglesey by surprise as well as by force.

The push into territory that was not yet part of the empire began the following season of AD 79. One must conclude that two legions at least, the Twentieth and Ninth, advanced from Carlisle and York respectively along western and eastern routes to Scotland, much as the trains do today. A legion on the march was a formidable presence. In front went lightly armed auxiliary foot-soldiers and archers, to look out for any sudden ambush, followed by the heavy cavalry and columns of infantry, and then the baggage train. Behind these came the auxiliary units, with more cavalry and infantry bringing up the rear. Somewhere in the middle were the legion's standard bearers, and the trumpeters and horn players. When on active service, Agricola himself rode up and down the line, encouraging stragglers and giving good marks for discipline.

The legionaries were impressive in themselves. Their regulation minimum height was 5ft 10in (1.78m or 6 Roman feet), and each man had to pass a medical test before enlisting. Recruits were put through courses of physical training which included route marches of 20 miles (32km) in five hours. They marched in step, six abreast, and on campaign might cover as much as 15 miles (24km) in a day, depending on the terrain and the circumstances. Their boots were thick-soled heavy sandals, studded with hob-nails with hollow heads and secured by leather straps wound up the shin. Wool or fur could be stuffed into the straps for warmth. It is unlikely that socks or stockings would have been any advantage in the Scottish climate. Well into the eighteenth century highland men and women went bare-legged and wore brogues, light, deerskin shoes whose uppers were punched with holes to let out water. The legionaries' sandals would have had the same effect.

The day's march can sometimes be calculated exactly from the distance between traces of temporary, or marching, camps (usually only visible from air photographs) believed to date from the same campaign – such was the intensity of military activity in northern Britain during the first three centuries AD, that more of these camps have been identified there than in the whole of the rest of the empire. Camps were of different sizes, designs, and proportions, with variations on the style of fortified gateway. A site at East Mid Lamberkin, just to the west of Perth, originally, at 1.02 acres (0.4ha), thought to be too small for a marching camp, has now, because of three different designs of gateway, been identified as likely to have been used for training.

Fortified camps were thrown up at the end of each day's march in a matter of hours, such was the command of logistics that governed their design and construction. The most basic defence comprised a broad V-shaped ditch with a depth of 3ft (1m), in front of a turf bank topped by wooden stakes, of which each legionary carried two as part of his kit. The men slept eight to a leather tent, carried by a mule; each tent community did its own cooking. The layout of the camp was like that of a miniature town, with streets separating neat lines of tents, and areas set aside for cooking, latrines, refuse pits, and officers' quarters. Each morning, the night's camp was dismantled, and the march resumed.

Describing this particular part of the campaign, Tacitus refers to no pitched battles, simply to Agricola's sudden spoiling raids, after which he would demonstrate the advantages of peace. As a result several tribes, or branches of tribes, who had up till then maintained their independence, handed over hostages and in return were given protection from their neighbours by means of a ring of manned forts. Tacitus adds, 'Nowhere before in Britain had such a transition been effected with so little interference from other tribesmen' (*Agricola* 20. 3). This suggests that in the territories occupied by the Selgovae and the Votadini, the main opposition on this occasion came from the mountainous terrain guarding the western approaches to the Highlands and from the weather.

It has been estimated that in the five years following Agricola's first advance beyond the Tyne–Solway line, Roman legionaries constructed over 35 permanent wooden forts of different sizes in southern Scotland. For these, local timber would have been used, especially oak from the mixed oak woods of the lowland areas. In these regions there had been massive forest clearance before the arrival of the Romans, as witness the amount of turf used for building fortifications, and the apparent ease with which sites on open ground were available for marching camps.

The forests, of pine and birch, began again as one moved north into the Highlands. The going, then, through and beyond the Borders by an eastern route, was easier than, for instance, in Germania.

The Scottish climate seems to have been much the same as it is today. Tacitus inserts an observation into his description of the Celtic tribes of Britain: 'The weather is foul, with incessant rain and fog' (*Agricola* 12. 3). Assuming this to be what his father-in-law, brought up on the French Riviera, told him, or wrote in a letter home, it sounds very like Scotland. The continuation, 'It doesn't, however, get terribly cold' (*Agricola* 12. 3), may refer to southern Britain. During the Scottish winters much of Agricola's army retired to winter quarters, often Carlisle (which enjoys the balmier breezes from the west, and where the officers' quarters may have been fitted with underfloor central heating), while the unfortunate on permanent garrison duties holed themselves up in their northern forts with enough supplies to last until the spring. The further observation, of the summer months, 'The nights are light, and in the far north so short that there is little distinction between twilight in the evening and morning; if there are no clouds in the way, you can see the glow of the sun all night' (*Agricola* 12. 3), embodies a clear reference to Scotland.

The Roman advance was accompanied by a programme of road building, to ensure lines of communication between military installations and across country, and to ease the way for subsequent campaigns. Roads followed the topography of the landscape or existing trackways, or were oriented by taking a line from a feature on the horizon with a surveying instrument called a *groma*. Initially the roads may have been little more than paths, but eventually there were at least 500 miles (800km) of metalled Roman roads in Scotland, with a milestone at each Roman mile. They were about 20ft (6m) wide, and constructed of crushed rocks and pebbles on a base of stones. A slight camber allowed water to drain off at each side. Normally the army did its own building and civil engineering, but there is a suggestion, in a speech Tacitus put into the mouth of the Celtic leader Calgacus, that in Scotland local forced labour was also used.

The Twentieth Legion, almost certainly under the command of Agricola himself, took the western route, which is followed by the present M74, to Crawford, where there are traces of a fort with wooden buildings and a rampart of turf. From there he turned north-east, to link up with the Ninth near Inveresk. That Agricola felt safe in bypassing the

Novantae in Galloway suggests that Petillius had already made contact with them on an exploratory expedition into Scotland from Carlisle. The route taken by the Ninth became the Roman road known from Anglo-Saxon times as Dere Street, which is followed for much of its length by the present A68. The establishment of the significant fort at Newstead (Trimontium) dates from this campaign – Trimontium means 'place of the three hills', a reference to the triple peaks of the Eildon Hills.

The Ninth Legion was at this time commanded by Gaius Caristanius Fronto, of a wealthy Roman family which probably settled in the colony of Antioch in the time of Augustus. He had commanded an auxiliary cavalry regiment from the Crimea, and was created a senator and then appointed a praetor under Vespasian. It is suggested that his wife was the daughter, or granddaughter, of the famous governor of Cyprus, Sergius Paulus, 'a prudent man, who called for Barnabas and Saul [Paul of Tarsus], and desired to hear the word of God' (*Acts* 13. 7). Caristanius left Britain in AD 80 to be governor of Pamphylia.

Vespasian died during that summer of AD 79. He was in his 70th year, and had been a hands–on emperor since AD 69. He had caught a fever while visiting Campania. When he got back to his summer residence, and place of birth, Reate, he made matters worse by continuing his regimen of taking a cold bath. He carried on working right to the end, insisting that an emperor must die on his feet. As he was dying, he joked, 'Oh my! I think I am becoming a god.'

The succession of Titus, now 38, was automatic. Only a few weeks later, Vesuvius erupted, engulfing two complete towns. Titus declared a state of emergency, established a relief fund for the homeless, to which he diverted the property of any who had died intestate, and appointed a team of commissioners to administer the disaster area. At the inaugural games which he sponsored the following year at the Colosseum, the great Flavian amphitheatre in Rome, 5,000 wild animals were slaughtered in a single day. The contemporary poet Martial records that among the other crowd-pullers was the spectacle of a convicted criminal being crucified while his exposed entrails were devoured by a she-bear specially imported from Scotland.

Clearly Titus's orders to Agricola were, as one might expect, to carry on the good work. It was the responsibility of the emperor to establish the boundaries of the empire. Roman policy was to mark a frontier not so much with a physical barrier such as a wall, but to establish a *limes* (plural *limites*), which originally meant simply a path between fields, from which it came to mean a boundary or frontier, often a military road linking permanent forts. The garrisons' responsibility was to discourage hostile groupings beyond the line, supervise the peaceful spread of Romanisation within it, and encourage trade across it. Uniquely in Britain, there could be no wholesale movement of peoples the other side of the frontier; the farther north it was set, the more the tribes beyond it were bottled up and in danger of losing their distinctive features. Archaeological evidence suggests that there was in ancient Scotland a cultural, if not also a political, divide between the tribes to the north and south of the Tay estuary. The northern tribes were being forced to fight to preserve their identity as well as their highland retreats.

At some point Agricola realised that because of the barren mountainous terrain, the lochs, and the jagged coastline, it was hopeless to try to tackle the north of Scotland by any western route. As in the previous year, he spent the winter of AD 79/80 dealing with administrative matters, probably from the provincial capital of London, reached from the north by carriage in five to six days. The following summer his combined column (now comprising detachments from all four legions and supporting auxiliary cohorts) negotiated the Forth estuary probably at Stirling and campaigned as far as the Tay estuary. Two temporary camps of almost identical size and shape at Dunning and Abernethy, a day's march (10 miles, 16km) apart, probably date to this stage of the campaign. They also illustrate the amount of disruption caused to the community simply by the amount of land needing to be cleared, in these cases 2,300 by 2,200ft (700 by 670m). The passing military even left their rubbish behind, to judge from fragments of Gaulish pottery discovered at the bottom of the ditch at Abernethy surrounding the camp.

This expedition, says Tacitus, 'brought [Agricola] into contact with new tribes' (the Venicones), 'whose lands he ravaged. Though the army was battered by summer storms, the opposition was so petrified with fear that they did not dare to attack. There was even time to build forts' (*Agricola* 22. 1). By 'ravaged' Tacitus could simply have meant that while the legions were on building duties they lived off the land, which would have been more seriously depleted of resources than if they were just passing through. What woodland there was supplied the timber, pastures were stripped of turf for fortifications, and farms and settlements forced to hand over wheat, barley, and livestock.

ORCADES

CORNAVII

SMERTAE

CAERENI

LUGI

CARNONACAE

DECANTAE

BORESTI

CREONES

CALEDONIANS

VACOMAGI

TAEXALI

VENICONES

EPIDII

VOTADINI

DAMNONII

ANAVIONENSES

SELGOVAE

NOVANTAE

7 Celtic tribes in Scotland, first century AD

According to Tacitus, during the following year (AD 81 by our reckoning) Agricola consolidated the gains made so far and embarked on an extensive programme of establishing military installations across the isthmus between the Clyde and Forth estuaries and covering the south shore of the Firth of Forth. Forts which can tentatively be identified as among these are at Barochan Hill, Cadder, Mollins, Castlecary, Camelon, Mumrills, and Elginhaugh. If the year AD 81, his third complete campaigning season, was originally to have been Agricola's last in office, as it normally would be, then it made good sense to call a permanent halt at such a point. This would enable Agricola, and the emperor, to claim the credit for conquering all of Britain that was seen as being worthwhile territory. Certainly the Highlands presented a singularly uninviting prospect.

If the line of forts represented the northernmost frontier of the Roman empire, one would have expected in addition a series of watchtowers, such as was the normal practice. Now there is just such a system about 24 miles (38km), a couple of days' march, to the north, the far side of the Ochils, a range of hills which continues along the south bank of the Tay estuary. The system is known as the Gask frontier. It is carried for part of its extent by the Gask Ridge, to the west of Perth, and it is still being excavated. The whole line runs roughly north–north–east from a point above Dunblane. It incorporates the Roman fort of Ardoch at Braco. From there it follows the Roman road to Muthill, where it turns east along the ridge, and then finally north-east at Finbo Gask towards Perth. So far discovered along its length of 23 miles (37km) are the traces of three forts, three fortlets, and 18 watch-towers, each of which was mounted on a square base and is estimated to have been about 30ft (10m) high. In design and construction, the watch-towers match those of the Wetterau *limes* in Germany, built in the first half of the second century AD.

That the Gask frontier is the first frontier system in Britain, and the oldest-known from the Roman empire, there seems no doubt. Other questions, however, such as when it was first constructed, and precisely what its purpose was, have not yet finally been answered. In some instances, too, the archaeological and historical evidence appear to be inconsistent with each other. On the one hand, it would seem logical to associate the original construction with Agricola's northern campaigns, while accepting that all installations north of the Forth were abandoned no later than AD 90. On the other, archaeological evidence points to some of the Gask watch-towers being rebuilt once or even twice, suggesting a lifespan of at least 15 years. This would take their initial construction back to the time of Frontinus, Petillius, or even Bolanus. One must bear in mind, however, that the construction of such a line must have had the express approval of the emperor. Bolanus, if indeed he did pursue Venutius into Scotland, was carrying out his original orders to try to resolve the Brigantian situation. In the chaos of and immediately following the year of the four emperors, there was no opportunity for any imperial instruction to do anything else. The historical evidence is that Frontinus was far too preoccupied with subduing and fortifying Wales, which he did not fully achieve, to be able to venture so far north.

Petillius was a personal favourite of Vespasian; he was also headstrong enough to be perfectly capable of acting first, and then getting the necessary permission. There is, too, as we have seen, archaeological evidence of his constructing military installations in southern Scotland. Could he have built the first Gask frontier, some 90 miles' (144km) march farther, through unknown territory, than he is believed to have penetrated? Certainly, two coins found in the vicinity by a gamekeeper in 2003, one on the site of the temporary camp at Mid East Lamberkin and the other in a field near Forteviot, could suggest a Roman presence in the early 70s.

On the other hand, the Gask frontier could not have been designed to stand on its own. It seems that it may have had several purposes, of which one was to back up with supplies, and with information communicated by signal, the series of Flavian 'glen-blocking' forts farther to the west and north: Drumquhassle, Menteith, Bochastle, Dalginross, Fendoch, Cargill, Cardean, Inverquharity, and Stracathro. Though the towers were still high enough to afford a view of the Highlands to the north, the installations along the Gask Ridge favour its southern slope, which suggests that their intention, apart from acting as frontier posts, was to monitor activities in the valley of the river Earn, which runs into the Firth of Tay along its southern bank.

While, given the available military manpower, a line of installations, or even two lines, with turf ramparts and wooden buildings, could be thrown up in a matter of weeks, planning and surveying would have been a major operation. None of this sounds like the work of Petillius.

To fit in with his two terms as consul in Rome, his three campaign seasons in Britain would have been AD 71, 72, and 73, of which the first at least was occupied by the problem of the Brigantes. While he may well have sited the original legionary fortress at Carlisle in 72 or 73, this hardly gives enough time for him to establish it as a base from which to proceed with his army on exploratory expeditions into southern Scotland, and to build frontier installations in unknown, and possibly unfriendly, territory. It would too have been military madness and political suicide to probe, and establish frontier lines on, borders verging onto the territory occupied by the Caledonians, while risking being cut off from the south if the Ordovices joined up with the Brigantes.

There is also the evidence of Tacitus that it was Agricola, not Petillius or anyone else, who first crossed the Clyde–Forth line. Tacitus, or the *Agricola*, has had a mixed press in recent years. The book was first published in AD 98. This was 25 years after Petillius's governorship, and only 18 years after Agricola reached the Tay. There would have been military tribunes from both campaigns now in the senate who would know the truth. Tacitus also was a senator, who had been *consul suffectus* in AD 97, and was now a leading advocate. Why should he risk his career and reputation by falsifying the record? Thus, until more conclusive archaeological information is available, Tacitus's general outline of events would seem to stand up to scrutiny.

Agricola was appointed by Vespasian but subsequently was answerable to Titus, whose decision it must have been to consolidate along the line between the Clyde and Forth estuaries. Titus died unexpectedly in September AD 81; some said he was poisoned by his brother. Traditionally, when an emperor died, all military campaigns were halted while commanders awaited orders from his successor. Agricola's master was now Domitian, who had hitherto played very little part in the administration of the empire, either to avoid any suspicion of nepotism or because his father and his elder brother (by almost 11 years) did not feel he was up to the task. It would therefore be a perfectly natural decision for him to confirm Agricola (who was a loyal Flavian and a safe pair of hands) as governor of Britain for a further term of three years, and maybe earn some glory for himself in the process.

Tacitus's account of Agricola's fourth complete campaign season (his fifth in all) opens with an enigma: 'Having crossed in the leading ship, he subdued hitherto unknown tribes in actions as successful as they were numerous. He drew up his forces on that part of the shore of Britain which faces Ireland, as a sign of intention rather than in anticipation of an attack' (*Agricola* 24. 1).

What did he cross? The 'shore of Britain which faces Ireland' must be the narrow peninsular known as the Rhinns of Galloway, from which the Irish coast can usually be seen clearly across the North Channel. The tribes, more likely tribesmen, were the Novantae – the Romans called the Rhinns *Novantarum Peninsula*. It follows that the crossing was from one side to the other of the Solway Firth, and that there was a reason for choosing this method of transport rather than going by land. If on this occasion the units of Agricola's army had wintered at York, rather than Carlisle, it would make sense to march to Alauna (Maryport) on the coast, and then cross the firth by ship. The most convenient landing place on the other side is the mouth of the river Nith. Here, at Ward Law, on a ridge with a fine view of the whole of the firth, are traces of a Roman fort which could be Flavian. Just to the south of the fort, the naturalist and traveller Thomas Pennant (1726–98) found in 1772 traces of a native hill-fort, surrounded by a double ditch and guarded on its south side by a steep slope down to the shore. In talking of an incursion into new territory, Tacitus tends to use stock phrases implying a plethora of individual battles. Might this hill-fort, however, have been the site of one such engagement? Tacitus may have been vague about the crossing either because he did not know where it took place, or because he did not think his readers would care.

The fact remains that the Novantae of Galloway were brought into the Roman empire at this time, but Ireland was not. To let Ireland go must have been a policy decision by Domitian, for Agricola was enthusiastic about the idea: 'Often I heard [Agricola] say that Ireland could be reduced and garrisoned by a single legion and some auxiliary units; also that it would be better for future relations with Britain, if the territory were to be ringed by Roman arms with no prospect of freedom' (Tacitus, *Agricola* 24.10).

The debate about whether there was at any time a Roman, or Romanised, incursion into Ireland still rages, but need not concern us here, except for a reference in the poet Juvenal (*c*.55–140), an exact contemporary of Tacitus, to having 'advanced our weapons beyond the shores of Ireland' (*Satires* II. 159–60). The poem was published after AD 116. If Agricola had made an expedition to Ireland, however, Tacitus would certainly have told us.

The evidence suggests that there were not many, if any, battles in Galloway that summer. Instead, there was a road-building programme which included what would appear to be a main route from Dalswinton west to the Rhinns of Galloway, terminating at Stranraer, at the head of the protected sea loch, Loch Ryan. This would have been Agricola's base for an invasion of Ireland. The fortlets at Glenlochar and Gatehouse of Fleet, along the route, almost certainly belong to this campaign, and the concentration of marching camps adjacent to Glenlochar suggests that on several occasions through the years Roman troops passed that way. North–south trunk roads were built from Carlisle to the Clyde and from Hexham to the Forth, linked by two main east–west routes, one of which may have had its western terminus at Irvine, suggesting a second sea base there.

There appears to have been no central tribal hierarchy in Galloway at this time. Small mixed-farming communities lived in settlements interspersed with brochs, crannogs (skilfully constructed by Celtic carpenters), hill-forts, and duns (round or oval stone forts). Their relationship to each other under the Novantian umbrella would have been similar to that of the clan sept. Contrary to the traditional view of the mercurial temperament of the Celtic tribes, the evidence of carbon dating suggests that anyway in the southern parts of Scotland formal fortifications had been in many cases abandoned before the arrival of the Romans, and thus that the tribes were now largely at peace with each other and within themselves. In lowland Scotland other than in Galloway, what had previously been hill-top forts were becoming hill-top towns, with room for several hundred families, an approach to urbanisation which had begun much earlier in southern Britain. The effect on these people of the march of just a single legion and attendant auxiliary units (say 7,000 men, 1,000 cavalry horses, and pack animals) would have been traumatic. The men and animals had to be fed and watered, and firewood obtained. Harvests would have been commandeered, grain stores raided, and stock depleted.

Agricola's whereabouts during the winter of AD 82/83 are bound up with a family matter. For in 83 he and Domitia had a son, their first child for 18 years, who only lived a few months. We may trust Tacitus's information on this matter, for the boy was his brother-in-law: 'At the beginning of the campaign season [of 84] Agricola was struck by a personal tragedy when he lost his son, born the previous year (*Agricola* 29. 1).'

It is interesting to speculate where and in what circumstances the baby was conceived. Wives did accompany their husbands on postings abroad, but not on campaign. Two factors, however, make it unlikely that Domitia was permanently in Britain during Agricola's terms as governor. The governor's palace in London, though planned at least from the time of Frontinus, was not ready for occupation until AD 80 at the earliest. And if Domitia and Agricola were cohabiting on a regular basis, even only during the winter seasons, one would have expected earlier pregnancies, about which Tacitus says nothing. For Domitia, unlike Agricola, was not in middle age. Augustus laid down that 12 was the minimum age for girls to marry, and most married between then and 15. This being so, Domitia would have been under 35 when the new baby was born.

The governor's palace was indeed a palatial building, a massive, centrally heated complex of halls, colonnades, offices, and domestic quarters. It may be that Domitia travelled to London to celebrate her husband moving into it with his personal and administrative staffs, and to enjoy its comforts, and the amenities and sights of the fast-growing city: the public baths (with their own water shaft), the amphitheatre, the forum, the basilica, and the docks. It may also be that Agricola travelled to Rome during that winter to consult his new emperor, or was recalled to Rome by Domitian for talks, and was able to take some home leave, during which the child was conceived.

Certainly the following year there was imperial initiative on two military fronts, and a change of policy in northern Britain. Domitian's personal project was to extend the German frontier at the upper Rhine, for which he would require 500 men from each of Agricola's four legions. In addition, he ordered Agricola to provide a further detachment of 1,000 men of the Ninth Legion to help cope with the Chatti, on the middle Rhine, who were raiding Roman territory. It would appear that in return Agricola was given permission to raise auxiliary companies in southern Britain; he was also provided with some conscripted auxiliary units from Germania, including a cohort from the Usipi, a tribe on the east bank of the Rhine not far from Frankfurt. Ireland was off the agenda. Having begun establishing a frontier along the Clyde–Forth isthmus, Agricola was now to push northwards, to promote the 'valour of our armies and the glory of the name of Rome' (Tacitus, *Agricola* 23. 1).

So, according to one of Tacitus's few specific locations, at the beginning of the season of AD 83 Agricola 'overran the people living on the other side of the Forth' (*Agricola* 25.1), that is the Venicones of Stirlingshire, Clackmannanshire, Perthshire, Fife, and Angus. Either he followed the line of march of 81 and made an incursion from the west, or he crossed the Forth at some point by bridging it. This would have been a simple task for his engineers.

Now for the difficult part of the campaign. Tacitus describes Agricola as meeting the initial challenge by simultaneously sending his fleet along the coast to reconnoitre and also to induce panic among the tribes, while his troops pressed on by the eastern route. That he followed the coast on this occasion is suggested by the fact that 'often infantry, cavalry, and naval personnel all met up at the same camp, where they messed together, cracked jokes, and boasted about their particular misfortunes' (*Agricola* 25. 1). Ptolemy refers to a base in this region called *Horrea Classis*, the 'Granaries of the Fleet', where corn could have been landed and stored for distribution to the troops and naval personnel during this particular campaign. A site at what later became the legionary fortress at Carpow has been suggested.

The northern tribes, comprising the Caledonians, Vacomagi, and Taexali, with perhaps some reinforcements from the far side of the Great Glen, were a totally different proposition to the more amenable, looser-knit societies to the south. Some kind of federation was agreed, under the overall banner of the Caledonians. These men were prepared to fight for peace on their own terms rather than the Roman version, and they included in their ranks less amenable refugees from the south who had come to make common cause with them. There was armed resistance and, Tacitus tells us, an attack on a fort or forts. That this happened on the Clyde–Forth line, behind the Roman line of march, is suggested by the fact that some of Agricola's advisers proposed a strategic withdrawal south of that line. He then had intelligence that the tribes intended a combined offensive in several columns. Conscious that he might be surrounded by superior numbers using their knowledge of the terrain, Agricola countered by advancing in three divisions. If each was represented by a single legion, the fourth being in reserve or on other duties, this meant that the vulnerable Ninth Legion, 1,500 men below strength, was on its own. Acting on their own intelligence, the Caledonians launched a night attack on the camp of the Ninth, overwhelmed the sentries, and forced their way in. According to Tacitus, the day was only saved by Agricola, who rushed to the rescue.

However far north Agricola penetrated on this occasion, it was too far to risk the decisive engagement before winter. His army retired to Carlisle, there no doubt to savour the most sensational news story of the season, of which there is a graphic account by Tacitus and a brief, but complementary, description in Cassius Dio. When one puts the two together, and fills in some historical details, this is what seems to have happened.

Some of the Usipi, conscripted in around AD 81 and posted to the east coast of Scotland, became fed up with being bullied by their Roman instructors, and mutinied. They murdered a centurion and several others, and hijacked three small warships, with their pilots. These ships, described as *liburnicae*, had two banks of 25 oars on either side, one man to each oar, with a sail fore and amidships, and could carry in addition a complement of marines. One of the pilots escaped, so the Usipi killed the other two in case they betrayed them. As they sailed northwards on their strange and erratic voyage, they were forced to land to take on water and supplies, antagonising local tribesmen. Eventually they took to eating each other. When they had finished off their weaker colleagues, they drew lots. Driven by oars, winds, and the tide, they sailed on, round the north coast of Britain, and stopped off at a number of forts on the east coast, where they escaped detection. They were finally wrecked off the north German coast, where they were mistaken for pirates and captured. Some who were sold into slavery ended up on the Roman side of the Rhine, where they regaled any who would listen with tales of their adventures.

It is said that their exploit provided Agricola with proof that Britain was an island, which gave him an idea that he later turned to good account.

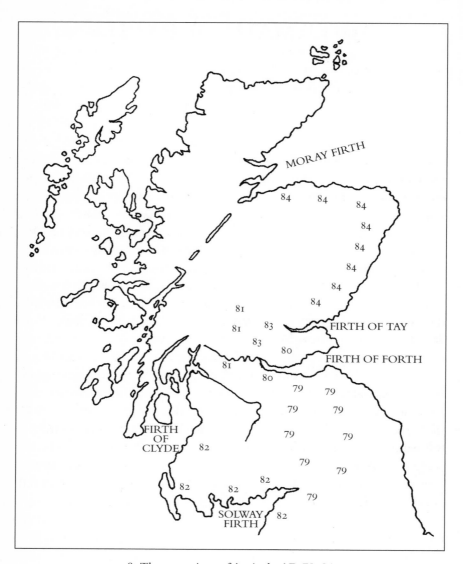

MORAY FIRTH

84   84   84
             84
             84
            84
         84
      84

81
81   83   FIRTH OF TAY
      83   80
81   80   FIRTH OF FORTH
         80
            79   79
            79   79
            79   79
FIRTH
OF   79
CLYDE   82
               79
            82
82   82   79
   SOLWAY 82
   FIRTH

8   The campaigns of Agricola, AD 79–84

5

AFTERMATH OF BATTLE

The question 'Who built what, and when?' is at no time more applicable in Scotland than in the decade or so leading up to AD 86. Tacitus states that the final stages of Agricola's military operation occurred when 'the season was now coming to an end' (*Agricola* 38. 2). He says nothing about what happened earlier in that campaign season of 84. It could be that installations north of the Clyde–Forth line were constructed at this time, and work begun on the most ambitious of them all, the legionary fortress at Inchtuthil. The Roman practice, however, where there was no initial surrender, was to bring a people to battle, defeat them, and then fortify their territory. If this was Agricola's (or Domitian's) policy too, we must look for another explanation.

Late in the summer of 84, then, Agricola sent his fleet ahead of him along the east coast, causing confusion and spreading fear among the coastal settlements. On this occasion the Caledonians foreswore their guerrilla tactics and prepared to tackle the Romans head on.

For the account of the battle of Mons Graupius, we are entirely in the hands of Tacitus, who omitted to give any indication as to where it actually took place. (Through an editorial error in one of the earliest printings of the *Agricola*, Mons Graupius, the Graupian mountain or hill, was spelt Mons Grampius, from which mistake we have the Grampians of today.) Theoretically, it could have been fought anywhere north of the Tay, and until there is conclusive evidence in the form of datable weapons or other traces, we shall not know the exact site. Practical considerations, however, suggest that it was within easy marching distance of the north-east coast. It has been inferred, from a line of marching camps which may or may not belong to this campaign, that Mons Graupius was either Mount Bennachie, or, farther north, Knock Hill, both of which have affinities with Tacitus's battlefield.

As with Agricola's crossing of the Solway Firth, it could be that Tacitus did not know the precise location of Mons Graupius, in a remote part, without roads, of a territory to which he had never been, or that he felt, with some justification, that his Roman readers would not be interested. We are on safer ground, however, allowing for the standard conventions of reportage of the time, with his account of the action.

On the slopes of Mons Graupius the Caledonian tribes gathered for battle.

Agricola's temporary base camp was near by. He marched his troops out carrying little more than their arms, and bivouacked for the night on the plain below the slopes. In the morning, as the tribes began to take up their positions, with more and more fighters still streaming in to join them, Agricola assessed the opposition: 'The front line was on the plain; the rest, rank upon rank up the slope of the hill, appeared to tower over the field of battle' (*Agricola* 35.3). Tacitus says that the Celts numbered 30,000, which may or may not be accurate. They would probably have included, apart from the Caledonians themselves, contingents of the Taexali of Buchan, Decantae of Cromarty, Creones of Moidart, Vacomagi of Badenoch, and possibly also members of the tribes farther to the west and north, the Carnonacae, Caereni, Cornavii, Smertae, and Lugi.

The proceedings opened with pep talks to the troops, such as are still a feature of modern warfare. In classical literature they reflect formal exercises in rhetoric. Tacitus puts the Caledonian point of view into the mouth of Calgacus, 'outstanding among the many leaders in courage and lineage' (*Agricola* 29. 4). He is not a king, nor a tribal chief, rather a vehicle for the political opinions of Tacitus and like-minded Romans. Calgacus is the epitome of the 'noble savage', happier in a natural state than in a civilised one, a theme which, in the hands of the social philosopher Jean-Jacques Rousseau (1712–78), had a remarkable influence on Western culture.

By demonstrating a united front, Calgacus is made to say, we can see off the threat of Rome and restore liberty to Britain. We, the last of the free, stand between the greed of Rome and its ultimate prize. 'They give the false name of empire to plunder, murder, and rape; they make a wilderness and call it peace' (*Agricola* 30. 5). He goes on to spell out the negative effects of Roman imperialism, such as slavery, taxation, and forced labour, and to emphasise the dissoluteness of the Roman nature. He ends with a rousing analysis of what the Roman ranks must be feeling at the moment, isolated in unfamiliar and threatening terrain. At which the excitable Celts raised cheer after cheer, mixed with chanting and ululation, and their lines began to fall into battle formation.

The name Calgacus means 'swordsman', which may simply be a title rather than an actual name. This is the only time that Tacitus, or anyone else, refers to him. If Calgacus had been killed or died as a result of the battle (as did Boudica), or survived and escaped (as did Bonnie Prince Charlie from the field of Culloden in 1746), or become a trophy prisoner-of-war (as did Caratacus and Vercingetorix), we should certainly have been told. Though Calgacus is generally believed to have existed, the question must remain whether Tacitus invented him for the purpose, just as he invented the words which he put into his mouth.

In Tacitus's account, Agricola now says his own few words of encouragement: a successful conclusion is their only chance of safety, and victory is a certainty. Now it was the Romans' turn to cheer.

There is little reason, however, to distrust Tacitus's description of the battle itself. Agricola had at his disposal three legions (each of about 5,000 men), eight cohorts of auxiliary light infantry (each of 1,000 men), and ten squadrons (500 strong) of auxiliary cavalry. The ubiquitous Batavians made up four of the infantry cohorts. The other six were also Celtic troops, two being from Tungria and the rest almost certainly recruited in Britain. Originally, auxiliary detachments were commanded by their own chiefs, but by this time they were led by young Roman citizens of equestrian rank, a *praefectus alae*, commander of a cavalry squadron, being senior to an infantry *praefectus cohortis*.

Unusually, Agricola kept his three regular legions (the heavy infantry), with four auxiliary cavalry squadrons, in reserve, posting them with their backs to the rampart of the makeshift camp where they had spent the night. In front of them he placed his auxiliary infantry, with the rest of the cavalry on their flanks. The legions lined up in three ranks eight men deep, each *signifer* holding aloft his century's standard, hung with medallions denoting battle honours. Beside each *signifer* was a trumpeter with his curved horn, whose principal duty during the battle was to draw the men's attention to their own standard. The red tunics of the legionaries, the plates of their flexible body armour, and their cylindrical shields contrasted with the chain mail and oval shields of the auxiliary detachments. The cavalry, similarly protected, were armed with thrusting spears. They rode without stirrups, on light horses no bigger than large ponies, with richly decorated leather harnesses.

While the Roman army moved into position, the Caledonian chariot division was noisily showing off its paces on the flat ground between
the two forces. As Agricola reconnoitred the situation, he realised that
the Caledonian front was so broad, and the ranks so deep, that a full
charge might outflank his line on either side. He therefore extended his
front by bringing forward some of the rear ranks. This made the line so
dangerously thin, that some of his staff officers pressed him to involve
the legions in the action. Agricola blithely ignored them and, in an
untypically headstrong gesture reminiscent of Caesar in his first battle in
Gaul in 58 BC, sent away his horse and prepared to lead his army on
foot from a position in front of the standards of the three legions, thus
denying himself an elevated view of the battlefield.

A legion's standard, the eagle, was its most prized possession, as well
as its rallying-point; to lose it was a national disgrace as well as a national disaster. All standard-bearers wore animal skins on top of their uniforms, a custom inherited from the Celts, with the head drawn up over
their helmets. A legion was divided into ten cohorts. At this time the
first cohort contained five centuries, each of 160 men; the other nine
cohorts consisted of six centuries of 80 men. There were thus 59 centurions in a Flavian legion, of which the senior, a post held for one year
at a time, commanded the first century of the first cohort, and was
known as *centurio primi pili*. The legionary standard was ultimately his
responsibility. There seems to have been no-one formally designated as
cohort commander, the function being undertaken on an *ad hoc* basis by
its senior centurion or by a tribune.

Agricola's personal staff on this occasion probably included the three
legionary legates (commanders) and the three legionary *praefecti castrorum*, career soldiers who technically ranked third-in-command of a
legion after the legate and the *tribunus laticlavius* (senior tribune of a
legion), but were more experienced in military matters than their superiors. Standing by, too, were the trumpet players, *tubicines* and *cornicines*,
who would convey Agricola's battle orders to the troops.

Then the battle proper began.

> At the opening of the first phase, both sides stood off and hurled their
> javelins and throwing spears. The Celts, bearing enormous swords and
> short shields, showed great composure and skill in ducking out of the
> way or fending off our missiles, while at the same time raining their own

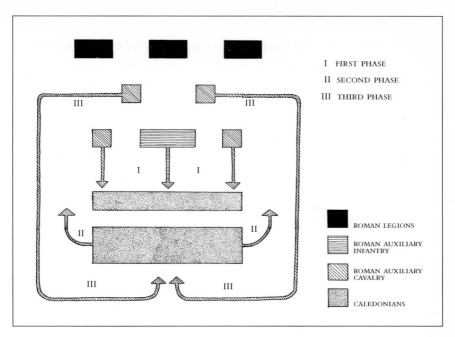

I FIRST PHASE
II SECOND PHASE
III THIRD PHASE

ROMAN LEGIONS

ROMAN AUXILIARY
INFANTRY

ROMAN AUXILIARY
CAVALRY

CALEDONIANS

9 The Battle of Mons Graupius, AD 84

down on us. Then Agricola ordered the four Batavian and two Tungrian
cohorts to advance and engage the enemy at close quarters with their
thrusting swords. These experienced troops were drilled in this form of
fighting, which the Celts were not used to. For their swords had no
points and were unsuitable in such a situation. The Batavians, striking out
indiscriminately with their swords and the bosses of their shields, and
stabbing the enemy in the face, overran the Celts on the flat, and pressed
on up the slope. At this the Tungrians took up the fight, and strenuous-
ly attacked their opposite numbers. The assault was over so quickly that
many of the enemy were left behind merely wounded or even unhurt.

Our cavalry squadrons, which had meanwhile dispersed the enemy
chariots, now joined in. Although the immediate effect was to instil
terror, our troops were finding it hard going on the uneven ground
against the massed enemy ranks. It was now hardly a cavalry operation
at all, with infantry struggling up the slope and being impeded by their
own horsemen, while empty chariots and terrified loose horses
careered into them from all sides.

The Celts farther up the hill, who had until then taken no part in the action and had had time contemptuously to observe how small our numbers were, now began gradually to move down the slope in an attempt to outflank the advance, wheel round, and attack from behind. Agricola, who had anticipated this manoeuvre, called up the four cavalry squadrons that he had kept back in case of emergency. So furiously did they charge against the oncoming opposition, that what was intended as a push forward disintegrated into a rout.

The tactics of the Celts now rebounded on them, as at Agricola's command the cavalry squadrons in the thick of the battle disengaged, rode round the packed enemy lines, and took the Celts in the rear.

Agricola 36–37

The carnage was terrific. So many prisoners were taken that some of them were butchered when more appealed to surrender. Others threw away their weapons and charged like berserks to their deaths. Those that got away and reached cover, turned and rallied, hoping to ambush their pursuers. Agricola had the woods surrounded, and sent in his light cavalry and infantry to flush out the fugitives. The chase went on until dark, when the Romans tired of slaughter and the survivors melted away into the wilds. According to Tacitus, 10,000 Caledonians died, against 360 auxiliary Roman troops. It would appear that not a single Roman citizen was killed, apart from Aulus Atticus, commanding a cavalry squadron, who, 'fired by youthful enthusiasm and propelled by the impetuosity of his horse, charged into the midst of the enemy' (*Agricola* 37. 6).

The Celts dispersed to the accompaniment of the keening of men and women, carrying away their wounded and crying out for survivors. They deserted their homes, setting them alight in their mortification, found hiding places, and immediately abandoned them, got together to try and make concerted plans, then suddenly went their separate ways. Sometimes they broke down at the sight of their own families; more often it drove them to fury. It was reliably established that some actually killed their wives and children, out of some kind of pity.

The next day revealed more clearly the extent of the victory. A desolate silence hung everywhere, the hills were empty, in the distance smoke rose from the houses. Our scouts saw no-one.

Agricola 38. 1–2

Having established that the Caledonians were not regrouping, Agricola led his victorious army down from the high ground into the territory of the Boresti. Clearly these people had not participated in the battle, for there was some kind of surrender, and Agricola 'took hostages' (*Agricola* 38. 3) as a pledge of cooperation. The identity of the Boresti has not been established, but they are believed to have inhabited a coastal district of Morayshire, where Agricola would have been able to link up with his fleet. That Moray coast has attained an additional significance since the discovery in the 1980s of traces of what would appear to be a line of wooden forts, each capable of housing an auxiliary cohort within its perimeter, at Boyndie, Thomshill, Balnageith, and Galcantray, and another one farther west at Tarradale. Each of these sites is adjacent to a river. The design of Thomshill has affinities with the Flavian forts at Barochan Hill, Fendoch, and Loudoun Hill.

At Galcantray there are traces of what would appear to be a timber gateway and a watch-tower, and remains which have been carbon-dated to AD 80–130. A suggestion of a watch-tower, rampart, and ditch showed up in an aerial survey of Tarradale in 1986. Subsequently iron nails were discovered on the site. Balnageith is not only situated at a suitable crossing-place of the river Findhorn, but commands Findhorn Bay, an ideal base for a fleet. Coins unearthed in nearby Forres in the eighteenth and nineteenth centuries carried heads of Vespasian, Titus, and Domitian.

Severe erosion as well as heavy agricultural activity have caused such damage to these sites that no conclusive proof of Agricolan activity has emerged. The balance of circumstantial evidence, however, would suggest that Agricola took the logical step of building such forts and installing garrisons in them, with the intention of maintaining a permanent military presence at the new northern extremity of the empire. Some of the forts might well have been in the territory of the Boresti; all the sites are on the best agricultural land in the area. Crop markings, however, come and go; evidence photographed from the air often cannot be confirmed on the ground. A familiar rectangular shape enclosing about 3.1 acres (1.3ha) with rounded corners has been spotted just to the west of Banff. Another, at Tearie, to the west of Forres, appears on a Luftwaffe reconnaissance photograph taken in September 1940, which subsequently fell into the hands of the Americans.

10 Scotland, AD 84–105, with places mentioned in chapter 5

As a final gesture of complete mastery over the whole island, Agricola ordered a unit of his fleet to circumnavigate Britain. Tacitus suggests that the complete voyage was done in one sailing, in an anticlockwise direction, starting and finishing at the same port, and making a formal landing on Orkney and sighting Shetland on the way. More likely, it ended at one of the ports on the west coast of Scotland.

There was still time for Agricola to retrace his march in a leisurely fashion, the more firmly to impress upon the tribes on his way that they were conquered peoples, before settling his troops in winter quarters, and himself returning to Rome at the end of his assignment.

Agricola had won just one major battle, by applying textbook methods, but had previously almost lost a legion. Domitian (now aged 33) had been completely overshadowed by the genuine military skills of his father and brother, which he was desperate to emulate. He had claimed a triumph for supposedly defeating the Chatti in AD 83, though ultimate victory did not come until 89. He had a jealous and suspicious disposition. Here now was Agricola, about to become a popular hero for comprehensively defeating, in the farthest corner of the earth, an army several times larger than his, and in the process securing for the empire a complete island province.

Under the circumstances, the emperor seems to have received Agricola's initial dispatch about his victory with some equanimity, though, according to Tacitus, when Agricola greeted Domitian in person, 'he was given a perfunctory kiss, and then, without a word, dismissed to join the crowd of imperial sycophants' (*Agricola* 40. 3). Agricola could not be granted a triumph (that was only for emperors), but he was awarded the *ornamenta triumphalia*, the triumphal regalia (the next best thing), a statue of himself crowned with a victor's wreath of laurel, and an encomium in the senate. Britain was, though, his last posting. When by reason of seniority he came up for election to the enviable job of governor of Asia, he declined, possibly because of ill health, which may have been brought on by the fact that Domitian had just had the previous incumbent executed. Tacitus records that the emperor, who had not exercised his discretion in offering a salary for the post, accepted Agricola's apologies 'without a blush' (*Agricola* 42. 2).

Agricola died on 23 August AD 93, at the age of 53, while Tacitus was abroad, where he had been serving for four years, probably first as a legionary commander and then as governor of a minor province.

From the apparently continuous visits to the house by Domitian's personal doctors and other staff, asking for news of the patient's condition, Tacitus suggests that the rumour that Agricola died of poisoning had some foundation. Whatever Agricola's military skills, he died, as he had lived, a career diplomat. In his will, he named Domitian as his co-heir, with his wife and daughter, hoping thus to ensure that they got something. As Tacitus comments tartly but with insight, 'So blind and warped was [Domitian's] mind by continual flattery, that he did not realise that a good father would not appoint an emperor a residuary legatee unless he was a bad emperor' (*Agricola* 43. 4).

We do not know the name of Agricola's successor as governor of Britain, or when he arrived, but on the face of it Agricola left him a stable political situation and the means, and plans, to consolidate the northern frontier. There could have been sound reasons for not after all encroaching into the Highlands. Communications were difficult – a comprehensive military road system such as Agricola had constructed in southern Scotland would not be in place for another 1,700 years. There were sparse resources – all the agricultural land in Scotland considered to be of top quality lies to the south of the Highland Line. A disproportionate number of policing stations would be required to oversee a scattered population. The preferred Roman policy of empire was to delegate local government to local officials where a suitable substructure existed. There was no such social structure in the Highlands at this time.

The installations north of the Clyde–Forth line served several purposes. That the 'glen-blocking' forts, which were not linked by any road, were intended to monitor what was happening in the glens seems more likely than that they were springboards for subsequent incursions into the Highlands. Indeed several of them are situated actually within the glen's mouth. There would seem to be further support for this view in that at Fendoch there are traces of a watch-tower, associated with the fort, on a hill a few hundred metres to the east. In 2002 the discovery was confirmed of traces of native roundhouses and a souterrain adjacent to the fort at Inverquharity, such as had already been found at Cardean. This suggests that even as far north as this the forts were for the few years of their existence in friendly territory.

The so-called 'glen-blocking' forts, designed to house one or more auxiliary cohorts, comprised a collection of buildings with walls of wattle and daub, surrounded by a rampart of turfs on a wooden base. The turfs were cut with a tool with a crescent-shaped metal head, such as is used for the purpose today. Along the Gask frontier, forts were interspersed with fortlets and the watch-towers. Since there are no signs of cooking in the watch-towers, it has been deduced that they were manned in shifts from a nearby fort or fortlet by personnel who brought packed meals with them.

The installations of the Gask frontier were linked by a road which appears to have continued to the fort at Cargill, and thus also to the most ambitious project of them all, the legionary fortress at Inchtuthil. The more conservative view is that Inchtuthil was planned, and work on the rest of the installations was begun, if not also finished, in the autumn of AD 84, to a blueprint prepared, before his recall to Rome, by Agricola in the light of his assessment of the situation with regard to the Highlands. In autumn, too, turfs are crisper than in summer and easier to lift. Some installations, however, notably Ardoch, Strageath, and Bertha, could equally well have been constructed by Agricola as outposts in friendly territory in the spring of 84, or even before that. It is also to be noted that as early a date as possible is consistent with the reconstruction of watch-towers on the Gask Ridge.

We are on firmer ground, however, with Inchtuthil. A legionary fortress was an essential component of any frontier system which bordered on hostile territory – there was at this time a positive concentration of fortresses along the west bank of the river Rhine, the natural border between the empire and Germania, and along the Danube, the border with Dacia. The fortress of Inchtuthil, intended probably as the base of the Twentieth Legion, was sited 3¾ miles (6km) south-west of Blairgowrie, between the present A9 and A93. The location may well have been chosen by Agricola or by surveyors working under his command, perhaps in the course of his march south after Mons Graupius. It was on the north bank of the river Tay, alongside the eastern route into and from the Highlands, while also guarding the entrance to glens which offered alternative, but more hazardous, movement each way. It was to be the crucial element in the northern strategy of the Roman empire. Its excavation in 1952–65 uncovered the most comprehensive ground plan of any Roman legionary fortress anywhere.

The fortress was defended by a ditch, 6ft 6in (2m) deep and 20ft (6.1m) wide, behind which was a castellated turf rampart about 19ft (6m) high and faced with stone on the outside, with a retaining wall of timber, and on top a walkway, 10ft (3m) wide. Within the defences was a ground space of 1,550 by 1,510ft (472 by 460m). The site would first have had to be cleared of trees and other vegetation, and then levelled. About a million turfs had to be lifted, transported, and settled in place, each measuring about 18 by 12in (45 by 30cm), and weighing about 66lb (30kg).

Except for the main bathhouse, all buildings were to be of timber, with tiled roofs. These included 66 barrack blocks, stores, workshops, administrative offices, eight granaries, separate houses for the commanding officer and senior staff, and a hospital (300 by 195ft, 91 by 59m) with 60 five-bedded wards. An aqueduct would have been required, bringing water from the hills, to meet the daily needs of the men and animals, and for the bathhouse and maybe also the latrines.

At Gourdie (also called Steed Stalls), just under 2 miles (3km) from the fortress, are traces of a smallish camp of 3.5 acres (1.5ha), probably used to house troops quarrying Strathmore building stone. The quarrying may actually have been done on the site. Other camps would have housed legionaries felling and processing timber, all of which could have come from within a 2 miles (3km) radius.

Estimates naturally vary as to how long would have been needed to build Inchtuthil from scratch. Much would depend on the number of men employed, the availability of supplies and materials, and the Scottish weather. Calculations suggest that it could have been largely finished by 1,000 legionaries working for 750 days in all, in other words in about two to three years. The fortress was, however, never completed. Only about 40 per cent of the work had been done when the site was abandoned and all structures carefully dismantled or destroyed to ensure that no use could be made of them by hostile elements in the community. The outer facings of the wall were taken apart stone by stone. Wattle frames of buildings were burned and the timber removed. Drains and sewers were filled with gravel or with finely pounded fragments of glass and earthenware. The whole contents of a pottery store were systematically smashed to pieces. A workshop's stock of 750,000 unused hand-forged iron nails, between 2in (5cm) and 16in (40cm) long with a total weight of almost 7 tons, was poured into a vast pit 13ft (4m) deep dug in the floor, and covered with a 6ft 6in (2m) layer of soil, which was packed hard down. Then the workshop itself was destroyed over it. The Roman historian Herodian (c.175–250), who wrote in Greek, described the tribes north of Hadrian's Wall as 'valuing [iron] as an ornament and a token of wealth in the way that other barbarians value gold' (*History*, tr. C. R. Whittaker, III. 14. 7). If this is so, then it would have been a disaster if this priceless cache of metal had become a valuable commercial commodity as well as the material from which weapons could be hammered out.

The nails were discovered in 1961. The outer layers of the hoard had fused into a solid coating. After almost 1,900 years, however, the nails inside their metal casing were virtually new, with clean-cut heads and edges, and bright patches of metal shining through a negligible coating of rust. The scientific explanation of this phenomenon seems to be that though the nails in the outer layers had corroded from the action of the oxygen in the groundwater, this process had removed the oxygen from the surround, leaving no corrosive element within. The lesson learned from this experience relates to the manufacture of safe nuclear-waste canisters which will protect their contents for at least a similar number of years.

The demolition of Inchtuthil was just one element in a planned Roman withdrawal, which archaeological evidence of coins, found on sites, places in AD 87 or 88. This would suggest that work on the site might not have begun until 86, 18 months after Agricola left but too soon for the complex of fortifications of which it is a part to have been designed by his successor. There is a mystery still about Cargill, where there are traces not only of a Flavian fort, but also of a Flavian fortlet. Which came first? The fort is too far north and too far from the entrance of the nearest glen mouth to have served as an outpost. It has therefore been suggested that the fortlet, guarding the bridge which carried the road to the fortress, is the earlier. Thus the fort would have been built as a precautionary measure once the decision to dismantle Inchtuthil was announced. In this case its brief life was thoroughly eventful, for there is evidence of its rampart having been repaired twice, once as a result of a fire which also damaged wooden buildings in its vicinity. The large, 8-acre (3.2ha) fort at Cardean, housing a cavalry as well as an infantry unit, also shows signs that its buildings and part of its defences were reconstructed.

The Caledonians may have lost the battle of Mons Graupius, but they had won the first phase of the war. Right across central and south-ern Scotland, the Romans destroyed or burned forts and other installa-tions before retreating. When Tacitus states sourly in the course of a catalogue of disasters in the west, 'Britain was completely overrun, and then immediately let go' (*Histories* 1. 2), he is referring to these events, for the area abandoned reflects almost precisely Agricola's conquests. The new frontier, to the north of the Cheviots, ran south-west from Newstead to Glenlochar, via Oakwood, Milton, and Dalswinton. It was, however, a theoretical frontier in that all these points lie in river valleys, and though there was access to north–south roads, it is not even clear that there was a road directly linking them across the intervening hills.

At the same time, defences were strengthened. At Glenlochar the existing fort was destroyed, and replaced by a larger one, probably to accommodate a double squadron of cavalry. At Dalswinton the fort was resited, and strengthened, and at Milton the defence works were completely reconstructed. The pivotal stronghold at Newstead, which was also the area administrative centre, was demolished and rebuilt to a new and enlarged design: in particular the width of the rampart was doubled to 45ft (13.7m), suggesting also a significant increase in height. It is possible that the fort at Loudoun Hill was maintained as an outstation, and to house troops on patrol in that area.

The decision to withdraw to the new line was forced on Domitian after heavy Roman defeats on the Danube frontier in AD 85 and 86 at the hands of Decebalus, king of Dacia. Though Decebalus was subsequently defeated, and a temporary treaty with him patched together, his German allies, the tribes Marcomanni, Quadi, and Suevi, were still a threat, and Domitian himself took the field against them in 89, and was defeated. To make good the losses of men and at the same time strengthen the Danube garrisons, Domitian transferred from Britain the Second Adiutrix and its auxiliary cavalry and infantry units. This removal from the province of one quarter of the available troops meant that it was no longer possible to sustain a presence in north Britain, and the Twentieth Legion was transferred to Chester.

The positioning of the refurbished forts, and their relationship with each other, suggest that the auxiliary troops stationed in southern Scotland acted primarily as security forces. Of the five main tribal groupings in the area, the Votadini, whose extensive hill-fort capital on Traprain Law flourished right through the Roman era, and the Damnonii are believed to have been pro-Roman from the start, and the Novantae, Selgovae, and Anavionenses (named after the river Anava, or Annan) to have accepted Roman rule. Such a situation had certain advantages to peoples who were less technologically advanced than the Romans, and had less understanding of law and government. They would not, however, have welcomed the requisitioning of foodstuffs and other produce at set prices, taxes in some form, a census, and the conscription of young men into the forces of the empire. Defeated tribes suffered the same indignities as those who submitted, under increased supervision. The alternative courses of action were to move out of reach of the military, or, as in the case of the tribes in the Highlands, stay out of reach.

Certainly, finds of first-century Roman items on native sites roughly coincide with the lowland region occupied by Agricola, and imply a friendly relationship between the two cultures. Likewise, there is evidence that, at Milton and Newstead at least, local men and women congregated for business and for barter. Oyster shells unearthed at Newstead are an illustration of one aspect of local trade: women's combs possibly another. The situation here would have paralleled that at Vindolanda, a timber fort on the Stanegate, the west–east road from the Solway Firth to Corbridge, from where Dere Street leads north to Trimontium. Vindolanda, occcupied from around AD 85 to 91 by the first cohort of Tungrian auxiliaries, and then until 105 by the ninth cohort of Batavians, was one of a chain of forts on the theoretical frontier between the client kingdom of the Brigantes and the tribes farther to the north. Personal letters, inventories, military reports, and accounts, written in ink on wooden tablets, have been excavated from Vindolanda, and give an insight into the garrison's activities on and off duty. A disparaging reference to the fighting capabilities of the 'little Brits' on a tablet (164) of the period 97–105 has been taken to refer to a batch of conscripts from the Anavionenses. The tablets also record, in addition to a consignment of oysters, cash purchases for the commander's household of ham, pork, roe-deer, venison, spices, beans, apples, honey, mulsum (a cooling drink made of white wine and honey), eggs, and chickens.

Domitian had been popular with the army for being the first emperor since Augustus to raise their pay. He had been so unpopular with almost everyone else that he became paranoid about conspiracy, reviving the imprecise charge of *maiestas* (treason) as an excuse for wholesale persecutions and executions. Unusually, however, his assassination in AD 96 was not politically motivated. It was organised by his ex-wife

Domitia, and carried out by a steward while Domitian was reading a report of yet another imaginary plot against him.

The senate was now able to make its own choice of emperor, which its members did wisely and well, appointing a 64-year-old distinguished lawyer, Marcus Cocceius Nerva, as head of state. Nerva brought the army over to his side by adopting as his son, and nominating as joint ruler and his successor, the commander in Upper Germany, Marcus Ulpius Trajanus (Trajan). When Nerva died in AD 98, Trajan was 46. He was an imaginative ruler, an exemplary employer, and a brilliant general, whose military exploits on the Danube and in Parthia left him little time to be concerned about the north British situation, or even where the northern frontier was.

In the summer of 105 the Batavian cohort at Vindolanda was transferred to the Danube front, for service in Trajan's second war against the Dacians. The order appears to have come at short notice, to judge from the signs of hasty, and in some respects unplanned, departure. Just before this, forts in southern Scotland had also been evacuated. This, too, may have been due to the Dacian wars, but something more sinister may be deduced from the fact that Glenlochar, Dalswinton, Oakwood, Newstead, and forts along Dere Street to the south, Cappuck and High Rochester, as far as Corbridge, suffered considerable fire damage at this time. At Newstead the buildings inside the fort were destroyed, and items considered too bulky, or heavy, or inconvenient to remove were buried in over 100 rubbish pits. These included an ornate brass cavalry parade-helmet and bronze face-mask worn on special occasions, table ware, bronze wine flagons, carpenters' tools, and spearheads, arrowheads, bolts, and swords. At Milton too, though there is no evidence of fire, the occupants of the fort seem to have left in a tearing hurry.

Whatever the significance of this involuntary withdrawal, it may have meant that the Selgovae and Anavionenses had rebelled against the administration, or that a new generation of the Celtic tribes from farther north had swept through the region seeking reprisals. If we include the incursion of Petillius, there had now been two Roman invasions of Scotland. Neither proved to be more than a temporary measure. The Romans would be back again, but not for another 40 years.

6

BETWEEN TWO WALLS

Trajan died on 8 August 117, at Selinus in Cilicia, where he had become ill on his way back to Rome from a campaign against the Parthians. He was almost 65, and he and his wife Pompeia Plotina had no children. On 9 August, Pompeia announced from Selinus that Trajan, on his deathbed, had adopted as his son Publius Aelius Hadrianus (Hadrian), commander of the army in Syria. On 11 August, the troops in Syria hailed Hadrian as emperor, rendering his acceptance by the senate a pure formality.

Hadrian was born in 76. His family emanated from Picenum, but had been settled in Spain for some 250 years, as too had Trajan's. The two families were related on the male side, and when Hadrian's father died in about 86, Trajan, Hadrian's first cousin once removed, and Acilius Attianus became the boy's guardians. Hadrian was an intellectual all-rounder who spoke better Greek than Latin, an exceptional soldier, an accomplished architect, a fine diplomat and politician, and a positive gallimaufry of opposites: 'He was, in one and the same person, austere and affable, solemn and sportive, hesitant and in a hurry, grasping and generous, devious and frank, cruel and kind, and constantly capricious in everything he did' (*Historia Augusta, Hadrian* XIV. 11). He was also tolerant of Christianity while exhibiting total insensitivity to the precepts of Judaism. In 100 he married Trajan's great-niece Vibia Sabina, who was ten years younger than he was. They had no children, but she is said to have procured a miscarriage rather than give birth to a monster such as Hadrian.

His accession as emperor was unopposed, but not without controversy. Cassius Dio, who was a consul, and twice a provincial governor, as well as a historian, claims that he had it from his father, who was at one time governor of Cilicia, that the news of Trajan's death was deliberately suppressed by Pompeia so that Hadrian's adoption might be announced first. It seems also that the senate was browbeaten, possibly by Acilius, into ordering the execution of four prominent politicians. Acilius at this time held the influential post of commander of the imperial guard, in which capacity he also had criminal jurisdiction as the emperor's representative. Three of the dead men were former or serving provincial governors, the other a former consul. All were close to Trajan, and might have been considered as his successor. Hadrian always denied that he had anything to do with these deaths, but from then on the senate regarded him with suspicion, which may or may not have contributed to his spending over half his years as emperor away from Rome, tirelessly travelling the provinces and the farthest frontiers of the empire.

Whatever problems he inherited from Trajan, two sources refer to disturbances in Britain. 'The Britons could not be held under Roman control' (*Historia Augusta, Hadrian* V. 2). 'As many [Roman soldiers] were killed by the Britons at the beginning of Hadrian's rule, as by the Jews' (Letter from Cornelius Fronto, a contemporary of Hadrian, to the emperor Lucius Verus, written in about 162). It is logical to link these actions with northern tribes, the same perhaps who created trouble early in the rule of Trajan. Whatever the nature of the revolt, it was put down in 118 by Quintus Pompeius Falco, who was governor of Britain from 118 to 122, though from an inscription and from coins issued in 119, it was Hadrian who took the credit! The problem seems to have flared up again a couple of years later, when detachments of about 3,000 troops from the legions in Germany and Spain were transferred to the north British front. They disembarked at Newcastle, where one unfortunate legionary lost his shield in the river, a crime equivalent, no doubt, to losing one's rifle today. The apparent disappearance from the records of the Ninth Legion at around this time is now thought to have no sinister implications. Between 108 and 122 it was transferred from York, first to Germany and then to the east, where it may have served in the Second Jewish War 132–5.

The emperor began his series of systematic and exhaustive imperial tours in 121:

> Hadrian travelled through one province after another, visiting the various regions and cities and inspecting all the garrisons and forts.

Some of these he removed to more desirable places, some he abol-
ished, and he also established some new ones. He personally viewed
and investigated absolutely everything, not merely the usual appur-
tenances of camps, such as weapons, engines, trenches, ramparts and
palisades, but also the private affairs of every one, both of the men
serving in the ranks and of the officers themselves – their lives, their
quarters and their habits – and he reformed and corrected in many
cases practices and arrangements for living that had become too luxurious. He drilled the men for every kind of battle, honouring some
and reproving others, and he taught them all what should be done.
And in order that they should be benefited by observing him, he
everywhere led a rigorous life and either walked or rode on horseback on all occasions, never once at this period setting foot in either
a chariot or a four-wheeled vehicle. He covered his head neither in
hot weather nor in cold, but alike amid German snows and under
scorching Egyptian suns he went about with his head bare. In fine,
both by his example and by his precepts he so trained and disciplined the whole military force throughout the entire empire that
even today the methods then introduced by him are the soldiers' law
of campaigning.

Cassius Dio, tr. Earnest Cary, *Roman History* LXIX. 9. 1–4

In 122 Hadrian crossed from Germany to Britain, 'where he made
many changes and was the first to build a wall, 80 [Roman] miles long,
which would separate the barbarians and the Romans' (*Historia Augusta,
Hadrian* XI. 2). He arrived at the northern frontier in June or early July,
bringing with him from the German station the new governor, Aulus
Platorius Nepos, who was a close associate of his, and a fresh legion, the
Sixth, either to replace the Ninth, or because he already had in mind
some intensive building work. Certainly the Vindolanda tablets suggest
that vast quantities of essential goods were being ordered at this time
from civilian suppliers. A letter (343) from one of these refers to 100
Roman pounds (518kg) of sinew, used as binding cords or catapult tor-
sions, 170 hides, and 5,000 pecks of ears of grain and 119 pecks of
threshed corn – it has been estimated that one peck of wheat represents
a subsistence calorie intake for one man for a week. Another tablet
(180), in the form of an account, lists a total of 320 pecks of wheat,
enough for 2,240 soldiers for a day.

Whoever wrote that account was dealing with various military personnel in the fort. He had also been in a bit of trouble. On the back of it he drafted a petition (344) to 'your majesty' (either Hadrian, who was known to be approachable, or Platorius Nepos), describing himself as a 'man from across the sea', that is, not one of your local riff-raff. Apparently a centurion had flogged him till he bled for supplying some substandard liquid, maybe wine or olive oil, and then added insult to injury by pouring it down the drain. With the fort commander on sick leave, the complainant had applied to the rest of the centurions and to the quartermaster, but they did not want to know. It would seem that he was not asking for compensation, merely official recognition that he was an innocent man.

Whether or not a final version of the petition was ever presented to him, in other respects Hadrian immediately got down to business. He either came to one of his quick decisions about the situation, or concluded that he had correctly assessed the reports of his military advisers. Hadrian's Wall is the most elaborate and, on the face of it, impregnable of Roman frontier systems, if it is a frontier system at all. As with many major architectural projects lasting a number of years, and work was still going on at Hadrian's death in 138, the plans were continually altered as building progressed. Hadrian was as interested in developing the economy of outposts of the empire as he was in defending it from attack. In Germany, before coming to Britain, he had developed the concept of the *limes* into a palisade of tree trunks 10ft (3m) high, set in a ditch; where the frontier crossed stony ground, the barrier was a dry-stone wall. This system was backed up by the standard watch-towers, signalling stations, and forts guarding the line. It was, however, hardly a deterrent to wholesale crossings, rather a method of controlling the flow. In Africa, which he may have first visited in 123, and where any trouble would come from cavalry rather than soldiers on foot, the defences comprised a broad ditch, 7ft 6in (2.3m) deep, and a wall 8ft (2.5m) high.

The mere fact that the nature of the defences represented by Hadrian's Wall developed over the years suggests a volatile political situation. The author of the biographical study of Hadrian in *Historia Augusta*, thought to be Aelius Spartianus, was writing about 150 years after Hadrian's death, but would have had more than just folklore to draw on. To separate the 'barbarians', by which is meant the tribes beyond the frontier, from the 'Romans', that is Roman citizens and denizens of the Roman empire, would constitute normal imperial boundary policy. To do so with a stone wall, 14ft (4.3m) high in places and between 28 and 33ft (8.5 and 10m) thick, supported by an intricate arrangement of ditches, ramparts, watch-towers, milecastles, and forts, argues a formidable situation on the ground.

The finished version comprised an integrated system of which the wall itself, of stone bonded with lime mortar, with a central core of concrete, stretched for 73 miles (117km) right across Britain from the new bridge across the Tyne (the Sixth Legion's first building project) westwards to Bowness-on-Solway, following, and to the north of, the line of the Stanegate. This was the narrowest part of Britain apart from the Clyde–Forth isthmus. Eleven forts, each capable of housing permanently an auxiliary cohort of 1,000 men, were positioned astride the wall at intervals of about half-a-day's march. Smaller forts (milecastles) abutted on to the south face of the wall at every Roman mile, each with a entrance from the south, and another through the wall itself. Between each milecastle were two watch-towers (turrets). The northern aspect of the defences was strengthened by a V-shaped ditch, about 33ft (10m) wide and 10ft (3m) deep, which in places had to be hacked out of the solid rock. There was a line of sight from the rampart which protected the walkway on the wall's top to the ditch, some 26ft (8m) from the wall. In a highly significant, and prescient, move, the line of forts, milecastles, and watch-towers was continued along the Solway southern shore and the west coast of Cumbria to provide a defence against nautical outflanking movements from Galloway or Ireland. That the threat from the west was seen as a reality is suggested also by the posting of auxiliary troops at outstations at Birrens, Netherby, and Bewcastle. These forts, in a line with one another about 8 miles (12km) north of the wall, were directly linked to the wall by road.

To the south of the wall was dug the Vallum, a continuous ditch supported on each side by a mound of earth, the whole structure being some 115ft (35m) wide. This was not so much a defence against attack from the rear as a means of restricting passage across the line of the wall to places where there was a fort, and of discouraging local tribesmen from building settlements except in the vicinity of the forts. In other words, there was deliberately created between the wall and the southern of the two mounds a no-go area for civilians, who had to cross the Vallum by bridge at specific control points.

There is some evidence which suggests that the territory of the Brigantes stretched into south-west Scotland, and thus that the wall, built for some of its length on prime agricultural ground, separated members of a tribe from each other. This would more readily explain the existence of the Roman outstations north of the wall. Though the wall itself could hardly have withstood a concerted attack from the north, it constituted a rallying point for the trained troops whose function it was to defend the empire against invasion. It would seem also as likely that it acted as a deterrent to troublemaking tribes to the north trying to link up with potential troublemakers among the Brigantes south of the wall, whose territory was still controlled by an unusual concentration of Roman forces.

The officer commanding the wall and its garrisons was stationed at the fort at Stanwix, on the wall itself just north of Carlisle. This was also the base of the *ala milleria*, a double squadron of auxiliary cavalry, of which only one was allocated to a province. Stanwix was situated on one of the two main roads to the north, and was linked to the legionary fortress at York by road, and by a signalling system using torches, which could spell out letters of the alphabet.

The original work of building the wall, milecastles, and turrets, and cutting the ditch (the forts were added during a second phase), was assigned to the Second Augusta, Sixth, and Twentieth legions, each working on a stretch of 5–6 Roman miles (8–9.6km) at a time. If local forced labour was employed, it would have been for carrying, not building. There was, however, backup from an unusual, and probably grudging, quarter, since naval units from the *classis Britannica* at Newcastle were drafted in to construct at least one of the standard stretches of wall, and a series of granaries. Subsequently, a special cohort of mixed cavalry and infantry was raised from naval personnel, which served as part of the forces patrolling the Cumbrian coast.

The sheer scale of the operation cannot be overestimated. Some 18,000 men had to be housed in temporary camps, and provided with rations and water. Where there was woodland, the trees had to be cleared to give a line of sight of several kilometres. Building stones were quarried locally in enormous quantities, and then cut, dressed, and hauled and levered into position. The stones were bonded with mortar prepared from local limestone, which was crushed and mixed with sand and water. Part of the wall in its original form was constructed of turf,

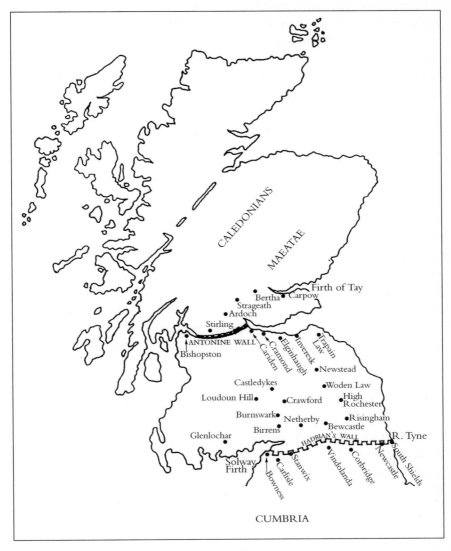

11 Scotland, first half of second century AD, with places mentioned in chapter 6

and its milecastles and turrets of turf and timber, which had to be cut and shaped. The rectangular forts, when they came to be built, were the work of the Sixth and Twentieth legions, with some details in the gateways being provided by the Second. Their area varied between 5 and 10 acres (2–4ha). The walls and principal buildings, administrative block, commander's residence, hospital, and bathhouse (usually sited outside the fort), were of stone: barracks, stables, and storehouses were constructed of timber.

When a legionary was not fighting or actually on the march, he was a manual labourer, and his centurion the foreman. The craftsmen and engineers of the legion would have done, or directed, the detailed work, some of which demonstrates individuality in design and construction. The surveyors laid out the course of the wall, and maybe also supervised the making up of its various elements. Someone, somewhere, must have exercised overall control. At the early stages, this would appear to have been Platorius Nepos. It has been suggested, from the archaeological evidence, that the lavish reconstruction of the Vindolanda fort at about this time, with oak beams, painted walls, and concrete floors, was to make it into his residence and headquarters. Platorius would have expected, on a reasonably long-term basis, accommodation matching that of the governor's palace in London. He was, however, replaced as governor in 125. According to *Historia Augusta*, there was at some point a spectacular falling out between Hadrian and Platorius. If this was connected with the building of the wall, then it may have been that the project was proceeding too slowly, or that it was already running over budget. We do not know the names of the two governors who followed Platorius. Sextus Julius Severus, one of Hadrian's most experienced generals, was appointed in 131, but was almost immediately transferred to Judaea, where he crushed the Jewish revolt.

Assuming that all building materials for Hadrian's Wall except specialist items were commandeered, the military personnel still had to be paid regularly, and they and their animals supplied with food. Legionaries were paid every four months, less standard amounts in the form of stoppages for rations, weapons, and boots. They also paid for their own replacement clothing. Higher grades, and possibly craftsmen and engineers too, were paid up to three times as much as a legionary. Centurions probably received five times a legionary's pay, and also benefited from the practice of taking bribes from the men for preferential treatment, such as lighter duties. Auxiliary troops were paid less than regulars, with the cavalry getting more than the infantry.

The Romans were capable of designing labour-saving devices, but, having plenty of labour available, whether provided by the army or by slaves, preferred to rely on their talent for organisation to achieve their architectural aims. One can only imagine the physical effort that went into the building of Hadrian's Wall, the inevitable injuries, and the resilience of the workforce in the prevailing weather – at one point the wall is 1,130ft (345m) above sea level, and at all higher reaches fog is a regular factor, to say nothing of driving rain and cold.

Garrison life, however, was less strenuous, at least for the officers, to judge from the Vindolanda tablets. The commander had his wife and children with him, and a full complement of slaves and other servants to attend to their personal needs, do the cooking and housework, and act as secretaries and tutors. They gave gourmet dinner parties, read books, wrote to their friends. There were officers' hunting expeditions, using hounds and nets to catch stags, swans, geese, ducks, and thrushes for the table. Shopping was done locally by slaves. More exotic items of foodstuffs, and tableware, clothing, and stylish curtains, were obtained by mail order through a supplier in London.

For the men, the routine would have been much the same as it is today: parades, kit inspections, fatigues, manoeuvres, training, sentry duty, route marches. A strength report (154) from Vindolanda, dated about the year 90, reveals that on that particular day, out of a total complement of 746 men and six centurions, only one centurion and 295 men were present, of whom 15 were off sick, six were classed as 'wounded', and ten were excused duty because of inflammation of the eyes (a very common complaint). Of the absentees, 337 and two centurions were at Corbridge, possibly on a training course, 46 were on special guard duties attending the legionary commander, one centurion was in London, another, with a squad of nine men, was in Gaul, possibly obtaining kit, and 11 men were away collecting the battalion's pay chest.

The bathhouse and the communal latrine were places for relaxation and conversation as well as for cleansing the body and defecating. The more energetic may have indulged in ball games, including a form of tennis played with the palm of the hand, as is fives today. Other off-duty pursuits included gambling with dice, board games (chess, draughts,

backgammon), and drinking and whoring in establishments which proliferated in the settlements round the forts. More permanent sexual
liaisons occurred, but the ban on soldiers marrying, introduced by
Augustus, was not lifted until the end of the second century. Leave was
not normally given to serving soldiers, but the Vindolanda tablets
include several obsequious requests to the commander for local leave,
which were presumably granted.

Hadrian's life was full of activity and spectacular achievement, of
which tangible evidence survives not only in the wall in Britain that
bears his name, but also the Pantheon in Rome, his villa in Tivoli, and
impressive remains in many other places to which his imperial tours
took him. It ended in loneliness and mental and physical deterioration.
Latterly he became so suspicious of anyone who was popular that several of his close associates were ordered to commit suicide, including his
89-year-old brother-in-law, Servianus. His wife pre-deceased him (he
was suspected of poisoning her), the youth Antinous, who was probably
his lover, drowned in mysterious circumstances on a Nile cruise, and the
handsome but feckless Ceionius Commodus, whom he had adopted as
his successor, died on 1 January 138. His next choice, a far more suitable one, was Titus Aurelius Fulvus Boionius Arrius Antoninus, now 51,
a distinguished politician and former governor of Asia, and the father of
two daughters. There were, however, strings attached. Antoninus must in
turn adopt as his joint heirs the seven-year-old son of Commodus,
Lucius Aelius Aurelius Commodus (later known as Lucius Verus), and
Marcus Aelius Aurelius Verus (later Marcus Aurelius), a 17-year-old stu-
dent of philosophy and the nephew of Antoninus's wife, Annia Galeria
Faustina (d. 141), whom Antoninus had married between 110 and 115.
After giving due consideration to the offer, Antoninus accepted.

Hadrian himself died at his villa on the Bay of Naples in July 138.
The senate, having nurtured its collective resentment for almost 21
years, proposed a motion to cancel all his acts, and withhold from him
the posthumous title of god. Antoninus objected, and had the deification of his adoptive father confirmed. It is said that it was for this that
he received the additional title of Pius – *pius* in Latin is not quite the
same as the English 'pious', having a meaning akin to 'dutiful' or
'respectful', especially to a parent.

Antoninus was an organiser with an eye to the economy, and preferred to govern the empire from its centre, Rome. It was said that his

aversion to travel farther than his estates in Campania was due to a reluctance to be a financial burden on the provinces. There was trouble in Mauretania, and in Achaea, Dacia, Egypt, and Germania, all of which was suppressed by provincial governors or military commanders on the spot. There was apparently trouble too on the north-west frontier, where 'Lollius Urbicus, his representative, conquered the Britons and, having swept the barbarians away, built a second wall, of turf' (*Historia Augusta, Antoninus Pius* V. 4). For these victories in Britain, Antoninus awarded himself a triumph in 143, and had commemorative coins issued carrying the symbolic figure of Britannia in martial gear.

So the Romans returned to Scotland in force. An inscription suggests that as early as 139 Lollius, newly appointed by Antoninus as governor of Britain, was carrying out an extensive building programme at Corbridge, where Dere Street begins. Since that fort was behind the line of Hadrian's Wall, and further reconstruction at this time is recorded at Risingham and High Rochester, along Dere Street farther to the north, this could only mean that a military push into Scotland was already on the cards very early in the rule of Antoninus.

Lollius, born in Africa, was a man of action who had served on the military staff of Hadrian during the revolt in Judaea in 132–5, and was subsequently governor of Lower Germany (that is, the northern German province). But was this incursion into Scotland of military necessity, or was it motivated by personal, political, or practical considerations?

The second-century Greek travel writer Pausanias states quite categorically that Antoninus never went willingly to war. This would seem to be confirmed by his biographer's summing up of his character: 'He was almost the only ruler of Rome who lived, insofar as it was possible for him to do so, completely without shedding the blood of citizen or enemy; he was rightly compared to Numa [first historical king of Rome], to whose fortunate disposition, piety, equanimity, and reverence he always adhered' (*Historia Augusta, Antoninus Pius* XIII. 4). Might there have been some disturbance in lowland Scotland which justified such aggression? Among volatile tribes who regarded themselves as separate units, 40 years is a long time to maintain a peace, however awkward. It is quite feasible that the Selgovae, or a tribe or tribes farther to the north, attacked and overran part of the territory occupied by the Votadini, who appealed to Rome for help.

It is also suggested that Antoninus needed an immediate military expansion of a high-profile province to bolster his position in Rome. He had been second choice as emperor, and he had no military experience. Such a campaign would give him the prestige he required to suppress jealousy from members of the senate who felt they also had a claim to the imperial throne, or who objected to his having interfered in the matter of Hadrian's deification.

Whether or not the Roman authorities knew of the existence of deposits of gold and copper that lay to the south of the Tay estuary, and particularly in south-west Scotland, it does not appear that they ever exploited these.

There may also have been a realisation that Hadrian's Wall had been built in the wrong place. It was now 60 years since Agricola had defeated the combined highland tribes. They had then been left to their own devices. It was a short enough time for resentment still to simmer, but also long enough for a resurgence of military resources. It was these tribes who presented a genuine threat to Roman interests in Britain, but geographically they were out of reach of strike forces based in the vicinity of Hadrian's Wall and farther south, and there was no way of containing them in their own environment, or even monitoring their activities.

Whatever the reason, or justification, detachments from all three legions marched out of their permanent bases, probably in 142, and advanced into southern Scotland: the Second from Caerleon, the Sixth from York, and the Twentieth from Chester. Evidence from marching camps suggests that they numbered about 16,500 men in all. They were on building duties again, and their objective was the Clyde–Forth line originally fortified by Agricola. It would make logistic as well as military sense to use both Agricola's routes through the Lowlands, even if the roads beyond Birrens and High Rochester may not have been kept in repair. It has also been suggested that the *classis Britannica* could simultaneously have sent ships along the east and west coasts to emphasise the Roman presence again, and perhaps also to deliver advance parties and supplies to the shores of the Clyde and Forth estuaries.

The effect of this incursion on the lowland tribes can only be imagined. The invaders were not auxiliary troops, or Celts, such as they were themselves. These were Roman citizens, professional soldiers who had volunteered for 25 years' service, and had been trained and disciplined to fight 'barbarians' whose attentions conflicted with the 'peaceful' administration of the empire. Maybe, as the *Historia Augusta* suggests, there was armed opposition. If so, it was put down in the manner graphically depicted in the reliefs on Trajan's column, erected in 113 during his lifetime to celebrate his victories over the Dacians and the acquisition of their territory as a province of the empire. Decapitated heads are held up to public display, prisoners-of-war are manhandled into the emperor's presence, and women and children, even a baby, are paraded for his inspection. The concentration of military sites of this period in the region occupied by the Selgovae does suggest that there was felt to be a danger of members of the tribe disrupting the building of the proposed wall.

Most of the countryside in which the Romans established their working camps and prepared to build the Antonine Wall had been cleared of much of the woodland and scrub by the Iron Age descendants of the original settlers. It was now principally pasturage, farmed peacefully but intensively by folk who inhabited settlements scattered over the landscape. The process of clearance had provided open space and all-important turf, but had largely eliminated the oak, the most durable wood for building, and birch, leaving the less suitable alder and willow in wet areas and hazel where the ground was drier. Local flowers, weeds, plants, and grasses proliferated in the semi-natural landscape. In the areas where there was further clearance of trees, bittersweet, bracken, and a variety of mosses grew up, with bluebells and red campions in the spring.

The precise location of the wall remained a mystery until the 1690s, when there was unearthed at Balmuildy part of a stone whose inscription linked the Second Legion with the governorship of Lollius – an excited antiquary, Alexander Gordon, called it the 'most invaluable Jewel of Antiquity, that ever was found in the Island of Britain'. It is now in the Hunterian Museum, with its complete inscription restored. Fragments of a second stone, recovered from the site in the twentieth century, also refer to building work by the Second Legion, under Lollius. We have no name of any subsequent governor until Papirius Aelianus, who is recorded as being in the post in 146. While various theories have been aired, it would make some sense for Lollius, supposing he took up office in 139, to be given two terms as governor (as had been Agricola), in order to complete the new frontier system, and to

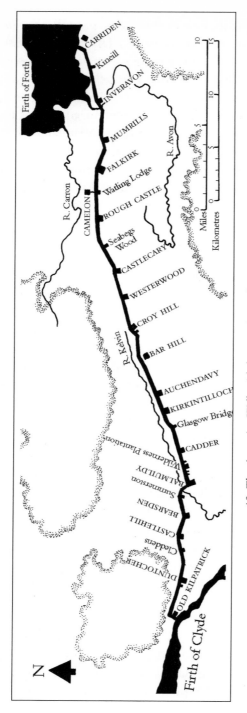

12 The Antonine Wall, with known sites – forts are in capitals

have been recalled in 144, though in the event the wall does not seem to have been finished for another six years after that. More invaluable jewels of antiquity have been coming to light ever since the seventeenth century, in the form of further inscribed and decorated slabs of local yellowish or grey sandstone. These carved distance-slabs, the largest recovered so far being 2.79m long by 1.19m high, with a depth of 0.15m, record who built which stretch of the wall.

The Antonine Wall was designed to serve much the same purpose as Hadrian's Wall, but built in a different place and from different materials. It marked the boundary between former barbarians and permanent barbarians, with facilities for passage between the two. Originally there were to be six forts along the 37 miles (60km) from the Clyde to the Forth estuaries, and these were built first, and presumably also provided some accommodation for the workforce, who up till then had been accommodated in temporary camps. Then work began on the wall itself, from east to west, with fortlets sited at regular intervals, through which travellers could pass from one side of the wall to the other. Each fortlet was supplied with cooking facilities, water, and a latrine, and was probably staffed by about 24 men at a time. Between each pair of fortlets were two watch-towers, manned probably by two men on duty, while the other six members of the squad rested in a shack one end of which was built into the south face of the wall.

The basic components of the defences included an outer mound, formed of the earth dug up from a vast V-shaped ditch, at most places about 40ft (12m) wide and 12ft (3.6m) deep. The ground between the ditch and the wall (a distance of between 20 and 30ft (6–9m)) was as an additional defensive measure pitted with an arrangement of rows of close-set oval holes, know as *lilia* from the pattern of a lily's petals. These can still be seen at Rough Castle, but they have also been found at several other points along the wall, suggesting that they ran its whole length. Two sharpened stakes, their points hardened in the fire, were driven into each hole, which was then partly filled up again to hold them upright.

The wall itself, on a base of stones about 14ft (4.3m) wide, kept in place by kerbstones shaped on site, sloped inwards from bottom to top for stability. It has been calculated to have been 10ft (3m) high, with a wooden palisade, or a wattle of willow and hazel, protecting the walkway along its top. To the south, along the whole length of the wall, ran a military road. While the wall was still being finished, the decision was made to increase the number of forts to 17. The new forts were smaller than the original ones and varied in size. Some of them replaced existing fortlets and reduced the number of crossing points. As with Hadrian's Wall, the purpose of the Antonine Wall was not so much to be the instrument of defence itself, but rather to act as a means of defending the province from attack and of monitoring the passage of travellers. It was just one element in an integrated system of defences covering southern Scotland, with outstations north of the wall at Camelon, and at Ardoch, Strageath, and Bertha, effectively enclosing the rich farmlands of Fife, and an intensified road network.

It has been calculated that 6,000 legionaries working full time could have dug the ditch and completed the wall in six months, in the course of which they would have stripped the turf off an area of about 900 acres (350ha) to make the building blocks, with an additional 100 acres (40ha) for the ramparts for the forts. The distance-slabs mounted into the face of the wall at each end of a stint gave, and in the case of the half of them which have been recovered still give, details of the construction. The three legions worked in turn to complete equal distances of between 3,000 and 4,652 paces (2,027–3,143m) for the initial stretch of 33 miles (53km). The final stretch of 4 miles (7km), from Castlehill to the Clyde, was divided into six shorter distances, recorded in Roman feet.

Less consideration seems to have been given than with Hadrian's Wall to the danger of being outflanked by sea. Though the successors to the Caledonians were formidable seamen, it may be that the Caledonians themselves had not yet found the means to combat the naval tactics first employed against them by Agricola. Forts were developed, however, as supply ports, of which Bishopton is the most likely candidate at the western end of the wall. In the east, Carriden, Cramond, and Inveresk were equipped with quays, and the development of civilian settlements around them suggests the existence of an additional workforce. The facilities in the settlement at Cramond at this time included a tannery. A Roman altar, dedicated to Jupiter, was found in 1956 outside the fort at Carriden while the land was being ploughed. The inscription states that it was put up by the villagers (*vicani*) of the fort. The status of *vicus* conferred official recognition on the village community, with sometimes also some powers of local self-government.

To the north of the wall, the reconstructed Agricolan forts at Camelon and Bertha were also on navigable rivers.

The forts guarding the Antonine Wall varied in shape and size. The administrative complex, the fort commander's house, and the granaries were usually stone buildings with tiled roofs. Barrack blocks, stores, and workshops had timber frames filled with wattle and daub, with thatched or slatted roofs. Each century (that is, 80 men) had a single-storey barrack block to themselves, partitioned so that each of the ten *contuberniae* (squads) had its own quarters. There were no central cooking facilities. Each *contubernia* did its own cooking, as it did on active service; it ground its own corn in a rotary quern, and baked its own bread. Every fort had at least one bathhouse, built of stone for the sake of safety. The bathhouse excavated at Bearsden was a miniature version of the municipal baths such as were to be found throughout the empire. The basic building is 100ft long by 16ft wide (30 by 5m), and comprises a series of rooms. In the first, you undressed, before going through into the cold room, off which, if you preferred, there was a sauna, with its own furnace, fired by wood or peat, and also a cold plunge. Otherwise, you proceeded, via two centrally-heated warm rooms, to the hot room at the end of the building, with an adjoining hot plunge. A stone path led to the inevitable communal latrine, which was flushed with used water from the bathhouse — since suitable sponges are not found in British waters, the occupants probably used moss to clean themselves. At Falkirk, a septic tank has been discovered outside the fort's wall, to intercept the solid waste; the liquid waste was then channelled into a sewer. Water for drinking as well as washing and other purposes was supplied by rainwater, or was drawn from wells inside the fort or from aqueducts which brought the flow from local hill-streams to the doorstep.

Evidence from inscriptions on building slabs, altars, or tombstones suggests that the basic garrison of each fort was 1,000 auxiliary infantry or 500 cavalry, mainly Celts, reinforced by small detachments of legionaries from the bases at York, Chester, and Caerleon. In addition, some of the original forts south of the wall were rebuilt, notably Newstead, where a detachment from the Twentieth Legion formed part of the garrison, Birrens, Castledykes, Crawford, Glenlochar, and Loudoun Hill. Other forts and fortlets were constructed from scratch. Suitable native hill-fort sites were converted for use as military training grounds. Woden Law, in Roxburghshire, is believed to have been used for the demonstration of siege techniques, and the nearby temporary camps at Pennymuir to have been where the trainees were put up in tents. The spectacular site on the summit and slopes of Burnswark Hill seems to have been employed as a firing range for slingshot, arrows, and mechanically-propelled missiles. There were in all some 50 military installations in southern Scotland during the Antonine period, with a total strength of about 21,000 men.

Archaeology can tell us something of how these men lived, and also what they ate, but only imagination can fill out the bare facts of serving on the edge of the known world in damp and cold conditions, cooped up with one's comrades-in-arms. The troops brought their own gods with them, and raised altars to them in the form of small, square pillars, for services rendered or prayers answered. Some men died while serving, the spot where their ashes were buried in a glass container or earthenware jar being marked by an inscribed gravestone, provided by the burial-club to which all personnel were obliged to contribute.

Pottery came in a wide range of shapes and sizes, the most recognisable being the glossy, red samian ware, mass-produced in Gaul and with a reputation for brittleness which may have been built into the design specifications. Cooking was done in jars and pots, some of them manufactured in southern Britain, and some actually in the forts themselves. Mixing bowls often had a layer of hard grit inside, to help the breaking-down process. Olive oil and wine came in amphorae, though beer was probably the soldiers' preferred tipple – according to the Vindolanda tablets the Batavians had a battalion brewer, and the Tungrians were supplied with Celtic beer in bulk. An inscription scratched on a piece of an amphora, found on the site of the third-century fortress at Carpow, is the first plant name in writing to be recorded in Scotland. It stands for white horehound, which, when mixed with wine, was said to relieve coughs and chest complaints, such as were doubtless an occupational hazard in the Scottish climate. It still used today as a homoeopathic remedy. Seeds of hemlock and henbane, employed as sedatives or painkillers, have been discovered at the mixed infantry and cavalry station at Elginhaugh. The Romans were much into medicinal plants and spices, especially those which added flavour or body to their cooking. Traces have been found in forts of this period of locally-grown pearl barley, and also common mallow (in the case of Bearsden, cultivated on the premises), and of imported coriander, dill, linseed, opium poppy, and wild celery.

The diet of the garrison at Bearsden has been analysed from the sewerage from the main latrine, which came to light when the site was being excavated in the 1970s. Cholesterol levels were at the lower end of the scale, suggesting a largely vegetarian diet. Two kinds of wheat were identified, emmer and spelt, the latter not grown in Scotland. A team of tasters concluded that bread made from hand-ground spelt, with yeast added, rose more and tasted better than a loaf made from modern bread wheat, while the emmer porridge compared very favourably with oatmeal porridge made in the Scottish manner. Traces of both wheats have been discovered in other forts on the Antonine Wall. Cargoes would have been unloaded into ox-wagons at the ports that supplied the garrisons, and delivered by road. With the grain came the grain pests, the grain weevil and saw-toothed grain beetle, and also the large ground beetle.

Other discoveries in the sewage included traces of lentils, beans, figs, hazel nuts, and wild fruits, the bilberry, blackberry, raspberry, and wild strawberry. Evidence from other forts along the wall suggests that some beef, lamb, pork, venison, and chicken were also eaten at times – sheep bones in large quantities were unearthed at Bar Hill. Some of the garrison at Bar Hill and Mumrills consumed mussels and oysters. Romans devoured large quantities of oysters, which may have been transported alive in tanks from the beds off the coasts in the south of Britain. Cheese was certainly eaten at Bar Hill and Castlecary, where cheese-making equipment has been identified. Ham or shoulder bacon, salted or pickled in its own brine, and vegetables would also have been on the menu, all washed down by beer (probably from malted barley) or sour wine. Among the vegetables introduced into Britain by the Romans are cabbage, endive, lettuce, and turnip.

Taking into account army dietary preferences, an auxiliary garrison's annual requirements of animals for food were quite modest, perhaps 20 cattle, 95 pigs, and 100 sheep. The cattle in the north of Britain were predominantly of the shorthorn variety. Sheep were lightly built, and resembled the Soay breed of St Kilda. Oxen, besides hauling wagons, provided meat, milk, butter, and cheese, as well as leather, bone, horn, and the ingredients of glue.

Cavalry horses were fed on barley, the staple Scottish crop at this time, and in winter hay from the surrounding meadows. Trade with local farmers would have produced cattle for sacrifices, and hide for clothing and shoes. Leather shoes for men, women, and children have been discovered at Bar Hill, suggesting the presence of the commander's family at least.

North of the wall, there are indications of trees beginning to reclaim agricultural land at about this time, and a marked drop in cultivation. If this was the case, this is more likely to have been a long-term effect of the losses of manpower at Mons Graupius than a short-term effect of troops living off the land.

In the area overseen by the Antonine Wall and its outstations, however, and in some other parts of southern Scotland, relations between the Romans and the local peoples seem to have been perfectly pleasant. Stone houses and other structures indicating wealth and status sprang up in the region between the two walls, and small settlements of four or five houses. Villages developed outside forts. That at Inveresk was bigger than the fort itself, with the east gate of the fort opening straight into its main street, which had side alleys running off it. The fact that some of the houses were rebuilt one or more times, suggests that the settlement was a permanent feature.

There was a similar situation at Newstead, an unusually large fort housing about 2,000 auxiliary infantry and cavalry. It was also the supply centre for all the Roman troops and military installations in Scotland, where iron smelting and lead working, and the manufacture of pottery, tiles, glasswork, and leather goods were undertaken. Outside the fort was a civilian industrial settlement with a population of about 1,000, to meet the needs of the military. Its inhabitants, however, do not appear on the whole to have been local people, but to have followed the army from the south. No evidence has been found of local artefacts or of local building techniques, and very few objects of Roman manufacture seem to have made their way into the settlement. The conclusions reached are that relations here between the two cultures were peaceable enough, but purely professional, and not particularly friendly.

The situation at Traprain Law, farther to the north, with its extensive settlement of hundreds of houses, seems to have been different. An abundance of Roman artefacts, including quality goods, and a corresponding lack of Roman military installations in the area, have been taken to suggest that the Votadini had a special relationship with Rome which ensured their freedom from unwanted tribal troublemaking. As long as the Romans remained in the region, the Votadini could have been regarded as a model power structure. An alternative view is that the site acted as host to crowds of visitors who came there to religious festivals, or even trade fairs.

Small quantities of quality Roman goods of this period have been discovered in the territories of the Damnonii and Novantae, including samian ware and other pottery, glass containers, beads, bracelets, and metalwork, some items being decorated with enamels of varying colours. These two tribes had common interests and building styles, especially reflected in their crannogs, and it would appear, in the same way as the Votadini, that their inclusion in the Roman empire was economically, politically, and socially advantageous to them.

A similar concentration of Roman artefacts is reflected in excavations of the brochs, hitherto known only in the far north, but which appear now in lowland Scotland. More than 15 of these monsters have been identified, in Angus, Fife, Perthshire, and Stirlingshire, north of the Clyde–Forth estuary in the region protected by the forts associated with the Antonine Wall, and across the south of Scotland from eastern Galloway to Berwickshire. All are in prominent or significant positions. Most were occupied in the middle of the second century AD. These structures are seen not as military installations, whether to combat the menace of the Romans or of unfriendly tribes, but as statements of authority and status within the community. As such they reflect the Roman provincial policy of devolved government.

7

RETREAT

Something happened between the walls during the years 154–8. A coin issued in 154 depicts on its reverse a dejected Britannia, suggesting a Roman military success. Several forts appear to have been abandoned at around this time, and then reoccupied. An inscription records that the fort at Birrens was rebuilt in 158, and archaeological evidence implies that it had previously been destroyed. Another inscription refers to repair work to Hadrian's Wall in the same year, which has been taken to mean that the intention was to recommission it as a principal frontier line.

Whatever the justification for the victory coin, it would appear that governor Gnaeus Julius Verus (155–8), either on his own initiative or, more likely, under instructions from Antoninus, ordered a retreat from the Antonine Wall which was then countermanded. In terms of the size of the province, the troops in Britain represented the largest garrison in the Roman empire, especially with the disembarkation at Newcastle and the return to their legions of detachments of the Second, Sixth, and Twentieth which had been sent to reinforce the armies in Germany. Even so, Julius Verus may have felt initially that they were spread too thinly over the ground, and that he could not afford to garrison Scotland any more; then he changed his mind, or had it changed for him by an emperor who was loath to surrender any of his military glory. Subsequent archaeological evidence suggests that there may have been no withdrawal at this juncture, and that the forts, including Birrens, were reconstructed to improve their facilities, or because they had been taken over by replacement troops with fresh notions of design. More economic use of manpower may have been the reason for some being abandoned altogether or, as in the case of Ardoch, reduced in size to accommodate a smaller garrison.

Antoninus Pius died on 7 March 161, in his 75th year, having overindulged in Alpine cheese. He had ruled wisely for 23 years, longer than anyone since Augustus, and on this occasion there was no controversy over the succession. Marcus Aurelius, of fine appearance and spotless character, was almost 40. Lucius Verus, whom Marcus insisted should share with him the office of emperor, was just 29. Marcus had in 145 married a daughter of Antoninus, also called Faustina, who had been born in 129 and was his first cousin. They had 13 children, several of whom died young. On becoming emperor, Marcus betrothed his 14-year-old daughter, Lucilla, to Lucius. They were married in 164. It was suggested that Marcus brought the ceremony forward because of Lucius's affair in the east with a trollop called Panthea.

Paradoxically, the 'philosopher emperor' was forced to spend most of the 19 years of his rule fighting first against the Parthians and then against the Germanic tribes, notably the Marcomanni and Quadi, who in 169 invaded Italy and besieged Aquileia. Lucius, with the help of some of Rome's most experienced generals, finally defeated the Parthians, but his victorious army returned with the most virulent plague (probably smallpox) ever experienced within the empire. He died in 169 while returning with Marcus from the northern front, to which they had gone with an army into which slaves had been drafted, such were the depredations of the plague and the losses and continuing military commitments in the east.

To sort out the problems in Britain, Marcus had sent Sextus Calpurnius Agrippa (162–5), whose presence there is attested by several inscriptions relating to Hadrian's Wall. We do not know who was governor when the momentous decision was taken finally to abandon the Antonine Wall. We do not know either precisely when the wall and most of the forts in southern Scotland were carefully dismantled and the retreat began to the comparative security of Hadrian's Wall. Archaeological evidence, taken alongside an assessment of the prevailing historical situation, now suggests, however, that it could have been in about 169, when the record states that, in addition to a massive coalition of hostile tribes 'from the frontier of Illyricum as far as Gaul', Rome faced 'threats of war in Parthia and Britain' (*Historia Augusta, Marcus [Aurelius]* XXII. 1).

The troubles in Scotland stemmed from the Caledonians and the Maeatae, the latter a new threat in their own right.

There are two principal races of the [north] Britons, the Caledonians and the Maeatae, and the names of the others have been merged in these two. The Maeatae live next to the cross-wall which cuts the island in half, and the Caledonians are beyond them. Both tribes inhabit wild and waterless mountains and desolate and swampy plains, and possess neither walls, cities, nor tilled fields, but live on their flocks, wild game, and certain fruits. . . . Their form of rule is democratic for the most part, and they are very fond of plundering; consequently they choose their boldest men as rulers. They go into battle in chariots, and have small, swift horses; there are also foot-soldiers, very swift in running and very firm in standing their ground. For arms they have a shield and a short spear, with a bronze apple attached to the end of the spear-shaft, so that when it is shaken it may clash and terrify the enemy; and they also have a dagger. They can endure hunger and cold and any kind of hardship; for they plunge into swamps and exist there for many days with only their heads above water, and in the forests they support themselves upon bark and roots, and for all emergencies they prepare a certain kind of food, the eating of a small portion of which, the size of a bean, prevents them from feeling either hunger or thirst.

Cassius Dio, tr. Earnest Cary, *Roman History* LXXVII. 12. 1–4

Though Cassius Dio incorporates this description into an account of a campaign that took place in 180, there seems no reason why it should not equally well refer to the situation in 169, when the Antonine Wall was still the principal frontier. Precisely who the Maeatae were, and this is the first reference to them, is less easy to explain. It is probable, however, that they were a new grouping of tribes, separate from the Caledonians. Their name has been translated as 'warriors', and places such as Dumyat (fort of the Maeatae) and Myot Hill in Stirlingshire would appear to confirm the territorial interests which Cassius Dio ascribes to them.

Whether the retreat took place in 169 or, as some evidence of coins and an inscribed altar at Castlecary suggest, a little later, it makes historical sense that it should have been Marcus Aurelius who ordered it. He desperately needed the extra men on his eastern and northern fronts, men, moreover, whom he could not afford to lose in a fruitless battle with the tribes in the north of Scotland. The existing defences along Hadrian's Wall were recommissioned and refurbished at this time, and a new military road constructed between the wall and the north mound of the Vallum. This tactic also put a buffer zone of tribes who had experienced over 25 years of Romanisation between the frontier and the hostile and aggressive Maeatae and Caledonians. To monitor this zone, and to give warning of trouble from the northern tribes, outposts were maintained at Birrens, Newstead, at that time the biggest fortified site in Scotland, and Risingham.

The care with which elements of the Antonine Wall were dismantled may be illustrated by the fact that of the estimated 42 distance-slabs originally mounted along its length in the 140s, 20 have so far turned up, the most recent in 1969. Of these, one has since disappeared, and two are incomplete, but the rest are in a remarkable state of preservation, having been buried in pits dug for the purpose. Some had subsequent histories before being handed over to a proper authority. A slab recording the work of the Sixth Legion at the west end of the wall, discovered in 1812, came into the hands of a Glasgow schoolmaster. After his death it passed to a relative, a weaver in Calton, who used it as a footrest. In 1824, it was rescued from obscurity by James Ewing of Strathleven, a West India merchant, who was subsequently lord provost of Glasgow and was elected to parliament in 1832 after the passing of the Scottish Reform Bill. He set it up conspicuously in a wall of his Queen Street mansion, which was later incorporated into Queen Street Station, where the stone became a landmark to generations of commuters. It was in 1942 finally presented to Glasgow Museum, now Glasgow Museum and Art Gallery, Kelvingrove. Another distance-slab is in the National Museum of Scotland, Edinburgh. The rest of the 15 more or less complete examples can be seen in the Hunterian Museum, Glasgow.

Other stonework was salvaged soon after the retreat by local people and used as building materials. The souterrain which survives at Crichton, Midlothian, has dressed Roman stones built into its walls, and a carved Pegasus, emblem of the Second Legion, on a stone in its roof. One can only speculate from where this prize trophy was lifted – Elginhaugh was the nearest Roman military installation, but the nearest significant presence of detachments of the Second Legion was at Newstead. Early in the eighteenth century three tombstones and two sculptured slabs came to light near Shirva, between the forts of Auchendavy and Bar Hill on the Antonine Wall. The tombstones record the deaths of a soldier from the Second Legion, a 15-year-old boy, and a woman. The slabs, depicting a woman in a carriage drawn by two mules, and reclining on a funeral couch, probably came from a monument to the wife of a fort commander. All these stones may subsequently have been used in the building of a souterrain actually in the ditch of the wall.

Before 180, the orderly retreat was complete. The frontier was once again Hadrian's Wall, this time for as long as there was still a Roman presence in Britain. The region left behind, unlike the rest of Britain to the south, was still devoid of towns and country estates such as the Romans contributed to other Celtic lands which had been annexed to the empire.

Meanwhile, in 175, Avidius Cassius, governor of Syria and a distinguished military man, had proclaimed himself emperor, having heard a false report of Marcus Aurelius's death. Marcus was forced to break off his continuing Germanic campaign to deal with the revolt, which petered out when Avidius was killed by those he thought were on his side. It was this demonstration of ambition on the part of Avidius that was responsible for Marcus having speedily to come to terms with the Iazyges on the Danube front. This tribe was holding, according to Cassius Dio, 100,000 Roman prisoners-of-war, which they now returned. As an additional part of the deal, probably as compensation for the prisoners who had already been sold into slavery or had died in captivity, they also surrendered 8,000 of their own cavalry, 5,500 of whom Marcus promptly dispatched to Britain. This does not necessarily mean that this was in response to a further military crisis on the north-western front, simply that this was the best available means, and Britain the best place, to train these former enemies and potential recalcitrants in Roman military methods.

Marcus Aurelius died in 180, having for the previous three years ruled the empire jointly with his erratic son, Commodus, now 19. Commodus had not been born to rule, but was named as heir apparent when he was five, and could hardly have seen his father except in the brief intervals between campaigns. This may have been his father's way of training him for the job. If so, it was largely unsuccessful, for Commodus demonstrated the nature of a latter-day Nero. The young hero, who showed at first some grasp of internal and external affairs, degenerated into a demented showman. He fought in the arena, defeating all his opponents (the fights were fixed), and from the safety of the stands butchered wild beasts and ostriches with javelins and arrow shots. He took the official title of Hercules, also a slayer of wild beasts, and in private dressed like the god. He was, however, generous with gifts, and the public at first adored him.

It must have been in his capacity as joint-emperor that Commodus sanctioned the appointment of Ulpius Marcellus to Britain, for a military certificate inscribed on metal names him as governor in 178.

> The greatest struggle was the one with the Britons. When the tribes in that island, crossing the wall that separated them from the Roman legions, proceeded to do much mischief and cut down a general with his troops, Commodus became alarmed but sent Ulpius Marcellus against them.
>
> Cassius Dio, tr. Earnest Cary, *Roman History* LXXIII. 8. 1–2

This time, the 'wall' to which the Roman historian refers must have been Hadrian's Wall. Was this, however, an armed demonstration by the previously docile tribes in southern Scotland, or a foretaste of what was to come from the mercurial, and to the Romans dangerous, alliance between the Caledonians and the Maeatae farther to the north?

Whichever it was, Ulpius, a career soldier, was regarded as the man for the job. Cassius Dio, who also served in office under Commodus, describes Ulpius as a martinet who kept his officers on their toes by writing out orders on 12 wooden tablets, which he had delivered at different times of the night, to make them think that he was permanently awake. He was as strict with himself, having his bread specially brought for him from Rome, not because he could not or would not eat local baking, but because by the time it arrived it was so stale that he was unable to eat more than was necessary to keep him alive; his intake was also restricted by the fact that he had sensitive gums, which bled if he ate anything hard.

> This man, who was temperate and frugal and always lived like a soldier in the matter of his food as well as in everything else when he was at war, was becoming haughty and arrogant; he was most conspicuously incorruptible, and yet was not of a pleasant or kindly nature... And he ruthlessly put down the barbarians of Britain.
>
> Cassius Dio, tr. Earnest Cary, *Roman History* LXXIII. 8. 3, 6

Whatever the nature of the uprising, it was not until 184, by which time we may assume that Ulpius had served two terms as governor, that Commodus was acclaimed as *imperator* for the victory, and took the title of Britannicus. Part at least of the campaign had been fought across southern Scotland. The forts that had been garrisoned as outposts, even Newstead, were abandoned, maybe lost in a Celtic onslaught. A mere 40 years since the comprehensive fortification of the Clyde–Forth line, there was now no permanent Roman presence whatsoever between Hadrian's Wall and the tribes in the Highlands. Another war had been fought, and won by the Romans, but the retreat from Scotland was complete.

There were other rumblings in Britain of discontent, this time from the army itself. Commodus had demonstrated his pathological suspicion of the senate by elevating favourites to positions of independent power. One of these was Tigidius Perennis, commander of the imperial guard, who took to making his own appointments, and to giving his son the credit for victories which others had won. The British legions, possibly also reacting against the extended ordeal of harsh discipline they had suffered under Ulpius, proposed to acclaim as emperor one of their legionary commanders, called Priscus. He declined. Perennis retaliated by removing all the commanders from their posts and replacing them with his own appointees, thus openly flouting the prerogative of the senate. There followed, if Cassius Dio is to be believed, an extraordinary demonstration by 1,500 ordinary soldiers from the British station. They travelled to Rome, where they lobbied Commodus and so cowed him that he believed their assurance that Perennis and his family were plotting against him. Commodus delivered up Perennis, his wife, his sister, and his two sons to the imperial guard for summary execution. Presumably, the deputation, their task accomplished by peaceful means, then returned to Britain.

Commodus now appointed Publius Helvidius Pertinax (126–93), another strict disciplinarian, as successor to Ulpius in Britain. Pertinax, the son of a freedman who ran a felt-maker's shop, had through graft as well as industriousness amassed several fortunes in the course of a series of governorships. He also had a fine record as a soldier, and had previously served in Britain as a military tribune.

Maybe it was because he became preoccupied with the problems inherent within the army that the tribes in Scotland were able meanwhile quietly to begin to organise a further campaign against what they clearly saw as the continuing threat of Rome. At first, Pertinax thought he had stamped out any signs of mutiny in the army, but the troops, having once enjoyed the experience of emperor-making, looked around for another candidate. They even approached Pertinax. Then there was a real revolt. One of the legions went on the rampage, and in the fighting Pertinax was badly injured and left among the dead. Having recovered, and succeeded in restoring order by exceptional brutality, he asked to be relieved of his post on the grounds of his unpopularity with the troops. He was posted back home, to be in charge of food grants for the poor throughout Italy. He then served as governor of Africa, before being appointed chief administrator of the city of Rome, where he was admirably positioned for the next round of musical thrones.

Cassius Dio was an eyewitness of what was happening in Rome. There was a recurrence of the plague, which took off 2,000 people each day in the city alone, plus many other unfortunates who died at the hands of a criminal element which had been paid to prick them with infected needles. This was, however, nothing to the pestilence that Commodus had become. No-one was safe, even members of his government, or his own valets, or his family – he had his wife and sister immured on the island of Capri, and then killed them. When he ran out of money to pay for his excesses in the amphitheatre and his largesses to the populace, he brought trumped up charges against prominent men and women, then had them killed for their property. Every senator, and his wife and children, had to give him two gold pieces on his birthday, and that was just for starters! He had the months of the year named after him, and statues of him as Hercules put up all over the city. Cassius Dio himself was one of the frightened senators forced to witness Commodus's antics in the ring during a fortnight of exceptionally bloody games; he records that he chewed on a laurel leaf from his wreath to disguise his nervous laughter.

Commodus was clearly mad, and it was only a matter of time before one of the many attempts on his life succeeded. It was planned by his valet and by Quintus Aemilius Laetus, commander of the imperial guard, for the last night of 192, Commodus having privately announced that he would execute both consuls for 193 on the first day of the new year. Commodus was to be killed by poison, administered in a beef dish by his mistress, but he vomited it up. So a professional gymnast of his acquaintance was sent in to strangle him in his bath. Commodus had ruled Rome on his own for almost 13 years. He was only 31. In a curious way, the manner and timing of his demise had a long-term effect on the emergence of a Scottish nation.

Before any announcement of Commodus's death could be made, associates of the conspirators approached Pertinax with the offer of the throne. Having sent a trusted aide to ensure that Commodus really was dead, Pertinax went secretly to the camp of the imperial guard. The men were initially alarmed at the appearance of the notorious disciplinarian, but he disarmed them with the offer of a cash bonus to each man equivalent to ten years' gross pay. He then dropped the first clanger of his brief rule: ' "There are many distressing circumstances, fellow-soldiers, in the present situation; but the rest with your help shall be set right again." ' (Cassius Dio, tr. Earnest Cary, *Roman History* LXXIV. 1. 3). The troops took this to mean that extra privileges given them by Commodus would be cancelled, and began among themselves to look around for an alternative candidate.

They murdered Pertinax three months later, and put the empire on the market to the highest bidder in terms of imperial hand-outs to themselves. The winner of this bizarre auction was a 60-year-old senator called Didius Julianus. There were, however, out of Rome, three other contenders, all army commanders with legions behind them: Lucius Septimius Severus (aged 47) in Pannonia, Pescennius Niger (about 58) in Syria, and Decius Clodius Albinus (about 48) in Britain, to which he had been posted by Commodus. Severus, a professional soldier who had been born in Leptis Magna, in the province of Africa, had the support also of the armies along the Rhine and the Danube, and thus had 16 legions loyal to him. Twelve days after the death of Pertinax, he had himself proclaimed emperor by his men. Niger, in Antioch, with ten legions at his disposal, was also saluted as emperor by his troops. Albinus had only three legions, but in addition could call on considerable auxiliary resources which may have included the remnants of the cavalry of the Iazyges. Severus was conscious of the threat to his western front, or to his rear if he engaged with Niger, should Albinus land his troops in Gaul. He therefore sent a deputation to Albinus, offering him the title of Caesar, which, since Severus's elder son, Bassianus, was only five, effectively made him Severus's successor. Albinus accepted, dubbing himself 'D. Clodius Septimius Albinus Caesar', and prudently remained where he was. Severus now marched on Rome.

In the city, the mob turned against Didius, and staged a sit-in in the Circus Maximus. The senate, having stripped Didius of office and condemned him to death, confirmed Severus as emperor. Severus reached the environs of Rome on 1 June 193, his men having marched 625 miles (1,000km) in under eight weeks. Before approaching the city itself, he paraded, and immediately disbanded, the imperial guard, which he replaced with men from his own legions. He entered Rome in civilian dress, having changed out of his cavalry uniform at the gates. Nevertheless, he was accompanied by armed men trailing behind them on the ground the standards of the former imperial guards, and by detachments from his legions, who found themselves billets wherever they could and commandeered food and other goods. Armed guards accompanied Severus to the senate house, where he justified his assumption of power on the grounds of self-defence after Didius had sent hired thugs to murder him, and promised vengeance and deification for Pertinax. He also proposed a bill to the effect that the emperor should not be allowed to put a senator to death without first consulting the senate, though, according to Cassius Dio, he immediately violated it himself.

While this was going on, his soldiers loudly demonstrated outside the building, threatening to strike if they were not paid a bonus equal to over eight years' pay, claiming that this was what Octavian's army had received for escorting him to Rome in 43 BC to take control as Julius Caesar's heir. Severus bargained with them, and they agreed to settle for one-tenth of their original demands.

A month after he had entered Rome, Severus left the affairs of the city in the hands of his lieutenants and 'set out to settle the situation in the east, still without saying anything publicly about Niger' (*Historia Augusta, Severus* VIII. 6). Secretly, he had secured the children of all the significant leaders in the east, except Niger's, who were still being sought. Niger was finally defeated early in 194 near Issus, and killed while trying to escape. Byzantium, which had been his centre of operations, refused to submit, even when Niger's head was paraded on a pike before the walls. The city held out for another year before surrendering; in reprisal, Severus had its walls knocked down.

There were still military problems to resolve in the east, which Severus partly achieved by annexing Mesopotamia. In the meantime, he had announced that he was the son of the deified Marcus Aurelius, and that Bassianus, now seven, should be known as Marcus Aurelius Antoninus and have the title of Caesar. This was a deliberate slight to Albinus, whom Severus knew was being invited by dissident members of the senate to come to Rome in the emperor's absence – Albinus came from a senatorial family in the province of Africa, and had an aristocratic upbringing. Now Severus sent to Britain a deputation of his closest associates, with dispatches for Albinus. These delivered, they were to say that they had additional secret information which they could only impart to him in private. When they had him alone, they were to kill him. If this failed, they had in their baggage doses of poison, which a cook or a cupbearer might be induced to administer. Albinus's security network became suspicious. The men were taken into custody and put to torture, under which they confessed.

Albinus's position, however, was untenable. In 195 he began to transfer his forces to the continent in preparation for civil war. It is likely that it was at this moment that he had his troops proclaim him as emperor. In Rome the establishment in the senate prevailed, and he was declared an enemy of the state.

While Severus was marching back from the east, Albinus was obtaining moral support from other aristocrats in Gaul and Spain, and military backing from Spain. He set up his headquarters in Lyons, from where he issued imperial coins emphasising his 'humanity' and 'fairness', and claiming that he had the 'confidence of the legions'. His troops won an encounter against the governor of Lower Germany, and generally ranged through Gaul. Cassius Dio illustrates the state of confusion in the region with the exploits of one Numerianus, a schoolmaster who gave up his job in Rome and went to Gaul, where he pretended to be a senator sent by Severus to raise an army. In this way he collected a small force, with which he made successful guerrilla attacks on Albinus's cavalry. Severus, believing Numerianus was a real senator, sent him commendatory dispatches, with orders to enlarge his force. Numerianus obliged, and among other booty sent to Severus 70 million sesterces which he had captured. When the war was over, he sought an audience with Severus, told him the truth, and, instead of demanding wealth and status, accepted a small house in the country and a modest pension.

Cassius Dio also claims that when the showdown took place in 197, there were 150,000 forces on each side. It is more likely that Albinus had just his three legions and perhaps 25,000 auxiliaries from Britain, plus some troops from Spain. Severus had at his disposal all the rest of the available forces, which would have totalled rather more than Cassius Dio's 150,000. The encounter took place at Tournous, 40 miles (64km) north of Lyons. Severus's right wing destroyed its opposite numbers, but his left wing was inveigled into an area honeycombed by *lilia*, those ingenious and potentially deadly oval pits such as had been employed to protect the Antonine Wall. As his men floundered about, Severus rode up, and was thrown off his horse. Albinus looked like winning the encounter, when a legionary commander named Julius Laetus threw his cavalry into the battle, and settled the issue. It was afterwards suggested that Laetus had deliberately held his force back, in the hope that both Albinus and Severus would be killed and the surviving troops on both sides would proclaim him emperor.

Severus's army sacked Lyons. Albinus committed suicide. His wife and children were killed on the orders of Severus, who had Albinus's head cut off and sent to Rome. He also exacted summary revenge on numerous prominent civilians in Gaul and Spain, women as well as men, who had supported Albinus, executing them and confiscating their property. Then he set out for Rome.

It would have been natural, with Britain denuded of its military forces, for the Caledonians and Maeatae in particular to have taken the opportunity of sweeping down from the north and causing havoc, but no conclusive archaeological evidence of such an incursion has been found. Instead, it seems that Albinus had come to some arrangement at least with the Caledonians, doubtless accompanied by massive bribes, that they would not cause trouble. As soon as he was able, Severus transferred Virius Lupus from the governorship of Lower Germany to that of Britain. Cassius Dio observes, 'Inasmuch as the Caledonians did not abide by their promises and had made ready to aid the Maeatae. . . Lupus was compelled to purchase peace from the Maeatae for a large sum; and he received a few captives' (*Roman History*, tr. Earnest Cary, LXXV. 5.4).

These hitherto un-Roman courses of action underline the problems which Lupus faced. For troops, he had the remnants of the Second, Sixth, and Twentieth legions and auxiliary cohorts which had fought for Albinus, and lost, together with whatever skeleton force had been left behind in Britain to keep the peace. Senior officers who had gone to war against the emperor would have been transferred, demoted, dismissed, or executed, and would have had to be replaced. A military campaign against the Caledonians and Maeatae combined, on their own terrain, must have seemed out of the question. Besides, there was other essential work to be done on refurbishing the defences of the province, where they had fallen into disrepair. The work appears to have begun immediately on installations in the Pennines some way south of Hadrian's Wall, and ended with repairs to the wall itself where parts had collapsed as a result of faulty building techniques. Improvements were made to fort facilities, and bathhouses which had suffered almost inevitable conflagration were rebuilt. A new provincial finance administrator was appointed, Sextus Varius Marcellus, presumably with instructions to overhaul the system and increase the revenue from taxes. Varius, a Syrian, had previously been in charge of aqueducts in Rome, but he was related to the emperor by marriage.

Back in Rome, Severus executed 29 senators without trial. They included Erucius Clarus, consul for 193, who was offered his life and a pardon in exchange for acting as an informer. Erucius refused, and was killed with the others. One Julianus accepted the role of informer in his place. He was set free, but only after being tortured to ensure that his evidence was the truth. The gymnast who had assassinated Commodus was thrown to the lions.

The confiscation of property ensured an influx of funds to the imperial treasury. Some of the money Severus spent constructively, by giving the army an increase in gross pay to match inflation, the first for over a hundred years. He also lifted the ban on soldiers getting married, which had stood for almost 200 years, and announced that permanent liaisons would be recognised as legal marriages. Then he left to resume his eastern wars.

He returned five years later in 202, having conquered Parthia, reorganised the eastern frontiers, and paid a state visit to Egypt. Almost immediately, he and his family departed on their travels again, this time to revisit Africa, the province of his birth. His return in 203 was celebrated by the dedication of the ceremonial arch, 68ft 6in (20.88m) high and 76ft 4in (23.27m) wide, which today still dominates the forum.

Quite what it was that determined Severus in 208, when he became 63, personally to lead a campaign to bring Scotland finally into the empire, is not clear, though both Cassius Dio and Herodian agree that he felt that his sons were becoming soft and unruly, and were in need of some military discipline. 'They outraged women and abused boys, they embezzled money, and made gladiators and charioteers their boon companions' (Cassius Dio, tr. Earnest Cary, *Roman History*, LXXVII. 7. 1). Antoninus, nicknamed by the people Caracalla, which means a Gaulish great-coat, was now 20. In 198 Severus had appointed him co-emperor, and had given his brother Geta, the younger by one year, the title of Caesar. The two siblings hated each other.

Cassius Dio further suggests that the troops on the continent of Europe were becoming slack through lack of action, and that Severus, 'though he was winning the wars in Britain through others' (*Roman History*, tr. Earnest Cary, LXVII. 10. 6), was utterly frustrated at being unable to arrest a notorious brigand and his band of six hundred men, who had for two years been ranging through Italy helping themselves to people's property and cash.

Herodian, who lived through these events and wrote them up in about 245–8, is more specific:

> The governor of Britain sent a dispatch to say that the barbarians of the province were in a state of rebellion, laying waste the countryside, carrying off plunder and wrecking almost everything. The governor requested, therefore, either that the garrison should be strengthened to give the province protection or that the emperor should come in person. This was welcome news for Severus, partly because he was a man who naturally liked glory in any case and wanted to win some victories in Britain.
>
> *History*, tr. C. R. Whittaker, III. 14. 1

The governor of Britain at this time was Lucius Alfenus Senecio. The two accounts are not inconsistent if the 'wars' that were being won were against the volatile Brigantes, and the 'barbarians' were the Caledonians and Maeatae. Herodian has, however, been accused of fantasising about the rebellion, of which no archaeological confirmation has been discovered. It may be that he introduced the governor's letter as a dramatic invention. Certainly his description of these barbarians and their land, which he had never visited, is based on fiction, folklore, and a scattering of literary references:

Most of [it] is marshland because it is flooded by the continual ocean tides. The barbarians usually swim in these swamps or run along in them, submerged up to the waist. Of course, they are practically naked and do not mind the mud because they are unfamiliar with the use of clothing. . . . They also tattoo their bodies with various patterns and pictures of all sorts of animals. Hence the reason why they do not wear clothes, so as not to cover the pictures on their bodies. . . . They are not familiar with the use of breast-plates and helmets, considering them to be an impediment to crossing the marshes. Because of the thick mist which rises from the marshes, the atmosphere in this region is always gloomy.

History, tr. C. R. Whittaker, III. 14. 6–8

The preparations for the campaign were on an unprecedented scale. To bolster the troops stationed in Britain, about whose efficacy and loyalty Severus may well have had doubts, he had as his personal escort the imperial guard. The total strength of this elite force, whose pay was twice that of the ordinary legions, was nine cohorts each of 1,000 men, with an accompanying cavalry squadron, *equites singulares Augusti*. It seems most probable that the army of invasion also included the new Second Legion (Parthica), raised by Severus for his eastern wars and now converted into a mobile strike force based in Italy. He certainly drafted in detachments from the armies on the Danube and the Rhine.

Even more significantly, the *classis Britannica* was on this occasion just one of four fleets involved, since the naval resources included also the two Danube fleets (a long haul for them) and the Rhine fleet. It seems likely that these ships were intended not only to ferry supplies to strategic points along the east coast of Scotland, but also to participate, as Agricola's had done, in a combined military and naval offensive.

Severus would for the most part take Agricola's route to the far north. There were extensive preparations on the ground. The fort at South Shields, at the mouth of the river Tyne, was converted into a major supply base, with 22 new granaries. The granaries at Corbridge were reconstructed and extended. Newstead was brought into service again. The military ports at Cramond and Carriden were recommissioned. The operational plan included the building of a fortress and supply base at Carpow, on the south bank of the Tay estuary, with

13 Scotland, AD 154–212, with places mentioned in chapter 7 and sites (marked x) of probable Severan marching camps north of the Forth

accommodation for 3,000 troops. Just behind Hadrian's Wall, there was a remarkable example of forethought. The fort at Vindolanda was razed to the ground and replaced by rows of circular stone huts, probably intended to house displaced persons from southern Scotland who were friendly to Rome, or else hostages from farther north.

Severus had with him his two sons, senatorial and military advisers, and an extensive staff of freedmen and others whose function it would be to help him run the empire from his tent. He also brought along his formidable Syrian-born wife, Julia Domna (*c.*170–217), who usually accompanied him on campaigns, in recognition of which she had in 195 been awarded the title of *mater castrorum* (camp mother). Possibly to avoid friction between the two brothers, or to give him some experience of administration, Geta was left on the Roman side of the wall with a team of senior advisors to administer justice there and to deal with matters of empire which came his way.

The evidence of the marching camps attributable to this campaign reveals the extent of the determination and threatening nature of the advance, as well as its progress. The southernmost, an enormous one of 165 acres (66ha), capable of holding 25–30,000 troops, is at Newstead, suggesting that this was the assembly point. Camps of a similar size have been detected between there and the Forth. The expedition then wheeled westwards, following the south bank of the Forth, which was probably crossed at Stirling, as it had been by Agricola. Beyond the Forth, the Romans were effectively in enemy territory. The size and siting of the marching camps immediately to the north of the Forth suggest that a garrison was left behind to guard the approaches to the isthmus.

At this point the army split into two divisions. One took the old Agricolan route traversing the mouths of the glens. The other turned eastwards along the south bank of the Tay estuary, which was probably crossed at Carpow over a pontoon bridge – coins of Caracalla dated 209 depict a bridge of boats, with the inscription '*trajectus*' (crossing over). This may well have been when work began on the fortress at Carpow, the initial construction being undertaken by elements of the Second and Sixth legions. This stone-built supply base, with permanent accommodation for half a legion, was to be the key installation in Severus's plan to conquer, and hold, the territory of the northern tribal federations. Immediately beyond the Tay estuary, the second division's march took them on a course between the first division and the coast. It has been conjectured that the two forces joined up again in the vicinity of Inverbervie.

Coins of 208 depict troops crossing a bridge, possibly the one across the Tyne built by the Sixth Legion, and also Severus, on horseback, leading his army into battle. The reality in 209 was somewhat different. Cassius Dio, who knew Severus personally, records that for most of the time the emperor was carried in a covered litter, being disabled by what was probably gout or severe arthritis. Beyond the territory of the Maeatae lay that of the Caledonians, regarded by the Romans as the guardians of the northern extremity of the island of Britain. Both Herodian and Cassius Dio have harsh things to say about the adverse conditions, which can be interpreted as woody and mountainous terrain, swamps, and the weather, and about the tactics of the opposition, which amounted to guerrilla warfare. Even so, Severus and his troops made it probably to the Moray Firth, where he forced the Caledonians 'to come to terms, on the condition that they should abandon a large part of their territory' (Cassius Dio, tr. Earnest Cary, *Roman History* LXXVII. 13. 4). Cassius Dio also states that Severus took along with him from Rome 'an immense amount of money' (*Roman History*, tr. Earnest Cary, LXXVII. 11. 2). Some of this, in the form of gold or silver, was no doubt paid over to the Caledonians on this occasion.

There was an incident as the Roman truce party went forward to meet their opposite numbers. Severus, on horseback on this occasion, in spite of the problems with his legs and feet, was riding beside his son when, according to Cassius Dio, Caracalla reined in his horse and drew his sword, as though to stab his father in the back. There was a shout from behind. Severus turned in his saddle, saw the sword, then simply proceeded in silence on his way. That night, however, there was a showdown in Severus's tent, but Caracalla was sent away just with a severe reprimand.

The whole expedition returned, to judge from the line of marching camps, by the western of the two routes through the territory of the Maeatae, and from there probably to York for the winter. Those detailed off for building work at Carpow would have remained on or near the site. Though Roman coins of 209 and the following two years glorify a victory in Britain, the advantage would seem to have gone to the Caledonians. Assuming that they received a large subsidy or bribe, the territory they surrendered was of little use to the Romans, who in any case seem promptly to have vacated it.

Before retiring to York, Severus took the opportunity of making a tour of inspection of Hadrian's Wall, where something rather alarming happened:

> After inspecting the wall at Carlisle, as Severus returned to the near-est guest house not only as victor over the Caledonians but also hav-ing established a permanent peace treaty, he wondered what omen would present itself. Just then, a black soldier, who was a well-known buffoon and regarded himself as a bit of a joker, came up to him with a wreath of cypress twigs. When Severus, thoroughly disturbed at being presented with a funeral garland and by someone of the colour associated with death, angrily ordered him to be removed from his sight, the man jocularly remarked, 'You have been everything, you have conquered everything, now may the conqueror be a god.' When Severus subsequently reached town, and wanted to perform a sacri-fice, owing to a mistake on the part of a local soothsayer, he was first taken to the temple of the goddess of war, and then supplied with sac-rificial animals that were black. He abandoned the sacrifice in disgust and retired to the local imperial residence, only to find himself, through the negligence of the temple attendants, pursued right to the door by the herd of black cows.
>
> *Historia Augusta, Severus* XXII. 4–7

Even for a Roman, Severus was hyper-superstitious. It may have been these and other recorded portents, as much as his own health, that convinced him to remain at York when in 210 the Maeatae made trouble in southern Scotland and the Caledonians broke the peace to join them in their campaign of violence against the state of Rome. Against them he sent Caracalla at the head of the army, with orders to slaughter anyone, man, woman, or child, that they came across. At the same time he raised Geta to the rank of Augustus, to be co-emperor with Caracalla and himself. Severus also made arrangements for the province of Britain to be divided into two, Upper and Lower, each with its own governor. The governor of Upper Britain, roughly equat-ing to southern England, the Midlands, and Wales, was to have his headquarters in London, and would command the Second and

Twentieth legions. His junior colleague would be based in York, and would have the Sixth Legion at his disposal. This reorganisation would ensure that for the time being no one man could command all the military resources of Britain.

As for Caracalla:

> [He] was not really interested in the war against the barbarians. Instead, he attempted to win over the loyalty of the army and began to induce them all to regard him alone as their leader, using every device to canvas for the position of sole emperor by slandering his brother. He regarded his father, who was suffering from a drawn-out illness and taking a long time to die, as a troublesome nuisance and tried to persuade his doctors and attendants to do him some mischief while they tended the old man, so as to get rid of him sooner.
>
> Herodian, tr. C. R. Whittaker, *History* III. 15. 1–2

Reading between the lines of both Herodian's and Cassius Dio's accounts of these events, it would appear that Caracalla returned for the winter of 210/211 without having achieved anything, whereupon Severus announced that he would personally lead the army out and into battle in the spring. He died, however, still in York, on 4 February 211, having counselled his sons, 'Get on with each other, pay the soldiers well, and treat everyone else with contempt' (Cassius Dio, *Roman History* LXXVII. 15. 2).

Caracalla was to observe to the letter the second and third exhortations, but neither he nor his brother took any notice of the first. Caracalla now dismissed the commander of the imperial guard and had numerous members of the imperial household executed, including, according to Herodian, the doctors who had refused to hasten the death of Severus. He then abandoned the northern campaign, and the region beyond Hadrian's Wall, having established some sort of peace agreement with the Caledonians and Maeatae.

The construction work at Carpow was never completed. While the extensive civilian settlement at Cramond continued to be occupied, a measure of the significance of the port facilities, the fort itself was evacuated, its dimensions of 532 by 463ft (162 by 141m) having remained constant throughout three occupations, two in the Antonine period and one under Severus. In 1997 a ferryman crossing the river Almond, which runs into the Forth alongside the remains of the fort, saw the head of a stone lioness glowering at him from beneath the surface of the water. When the statue, 5ft (1.5m) long and weighing 1½ tons, had been extricated from the mud, it was identified as the top part of a tomb, probably of a fort commander, dating to the Severan period. No other Roman sculptured lioness has been found in Britain, nor anywhere one that is in the process of eating a man, whose bearded head is being drawn back into the creature's jaws between her front paws. The city of Edinburgh and the National Museums of Scotland now own the lioness jointly, and the ferryman received a reward of £50,000.

Caracalla and Geta did not speak to each other on the journey back to Rome with their mother, and subsequently spent much time and effort trying to poison each other. Any other method was likely to fail as each was closely attended by soldiers and by beefy personal body-guards. Finally, towards the end of December 212, Caracalla persuaded Julia Domna to invite them both to a private meeting of reconciliation in her apartment. When all three were closeted together, in rushed a couple of centurions, who stabbed Geta to death in his mother's arms. Caracalla then ran post haste to the imperial guards' camp, where he claimed that there had been an attempt on his life and promised the troops extensive favours. In the senate the next day he offered amnesties to political opponents and exiles, and urged everyone to rally behind a single emperor. Then he set about killing all those who had been even casually acquainted with Geta – men, women, and children. Cassius Dio records that 20,000 died.

The army, however, loved him, because he acted the ranker and even marched among them on campaign, and because, in line with his father's deathbed advice, he twice increased their pay. This, however, initiated a financial crisis, which Caracalla attempted to redress by granting Roman citizenship to all free inhabitants of the empire, thus rendering them eligible for taxation, the rate of which was doubled. The process of universal enfranchisement had begun in the third century BC; Caracalla may be credited with completing it. Whatever his motive, the empire was now theoretically a recognisable commonwealth of peoples. His action may, however, have given the necessary impetus to those immediately outside the frontiers of the empire, such as were the Caledonians and Maeatae, to unite against the age-old enemy who had wantonly invaded their territory for a fourth time.

8

PICT AND SCOT

Caracalla, while campaigning in the east in 217, was assassinated by a detachment of his own imperial guard, probably on the instructions of their commander, Marcus Opellius Macrinus (c.165–218), who had nothing to lose. For Caracalla, having learned from a soothsayer that Macrinus would become emperor, had been reassigning his staff to other posts, preparatory to having him killed. Macrinus, with the acquiescence of the senate, now took office.

Extraordinarily, the uneasy peace which Severus had negotiated with the tribes in the far north of Britain seems to have been maintained for almost a century after Caracalla's death. Two features of the Severan treatment of the tribes and reorganisation of the administration of the region north of Hadrian's Wall have been suggested as contributing to this comparative state of calm.

Several hoards of Roman coins dating to this period or soon afterwards which have been unearthed in various parts of Scotland testify to the policy, such as circumstances had forced upon Virius Lupus, of paying bribes to the native population. Roman coins do not carry dates, which were calculated from the foundation of the city, but the date of issue can often be ascertained by the number of consulships attributed to the emperor or times he had been acclaimed as *imperator*, and by other identifiable factors such as a victory celebration. In 2000 and 2001 two hoards of Roman silver *denarii* in local earthenware pots were unearthed within 10m of each other in the course of the excavation of an Iron Age settlement at Birnie, north Morayshire. One comprised 313 coins, the other 310, each roughly amounting to a year's gross pay for a legionary. They date from AD 60 in the reign of Nero to AD 197, that is some years before Severus arrived in Scotland.

The range of dates would seem to make it unlikely that this was loot collected on a raid across the frontier some 200 miles (320km) away. The terminal date coincides with Virius Lupus's arrival in Britain and his buying off the Maeatae, and possibly also the Caledonians, within whose former territory these hoards were found. Celts in Scotland did not at this time use money, but bartered for goods. The hoards may each represent a family's individual allocation from the pool, kept for reasons of status or as a means of bargaining, and then buried at a time of crisis or as an offering to a local deity. A larger cache, of almost 2,000 *denarii*, was buried at Falkirk, adjacent to the abandoned Antonine Wall, in or shortly after 235, suggesting a continuation of the policy of bribes for peace.

The other feature involved the establishment of an elaborate policing system of the lowland region at least as far as the Forth. The outpost forts of Birrens, Netherby, and Bewcastle were rebuilt, and the forts at Risingham, High Rochester, and Cappuck on Dere Street, the eastern main road into Scotland, were brought back into service. Each of these may have housed a permanent garrison of 1,000 mixed infantry and cavalry. They also acted as temporary headquarters for members of a new force called *exploratores* (frontier scouts) – according to the *Antonine Itinerary*, a geographical guide compiled in the time of Caracalla between 212 and 216, Netherby was known as *Castra Exploratorum* (Scouts' Camp). There is no suggestion that at this time these men were spies. Their function would have been to act over a wide area as security forces, patrolling the pathways, keeping the peace, and always on alert to give advance warning of any trouble from the northern tribes, between whom and Hadrian's Wall there was now once more an operational buffer zone.

The precise relationship between the individual lowland tribes and the Romans at this time can only be guessed at. The Votadini stronghold at Traprain Law continued to be a centre for manufacturing and trade. If the evidence from hill-fort sites in south-east Scotland, territory of the Votadini and Selgovae, suggests that fort installations were replaced by stone settlement buildings, which it would seem to do, then this would confirm that communities there now lived without fear of attack. It is probable that there was some kind of treaty with the southern tribes such as Cassius Dio describes as being established by Commodus in 180 with the Marcomanni and

Quadi, two Germanic tribes immediately outside the frontiers of the empire. The region would have been equivalent to a protectorate supervised by the outpost troops and *exploratores*. The tribes were relieved of the burden of paying taxes, though they would probably still have to supply manpower for the army of Rome, when there were not enough volunteers. Where local tribesmen were discouraged from looting their neighbours, the army offered an alternative way of making a living.

The Roman treaty with the Marcomanni established that 'they should not assemble often nor in many parts of the country, but only once each month and in one place, and in the presence of a Roman centurion' (Cassius Dio, tr. Earnest Cary, *Roman History* LXXIII. 2. 4). That a similar system operated in southern Scotland, there would seem to be evidence from an ingenious but authoritative interpretation of a section in the *Ravenna Cosmography*, a seventh-century compilation in Latin of geographical names, mainly taken from Roman road maps:'There are, however, in Britain itself various places (*loca*), several of which we wish to mention: Maponi, Mixa, Panovius, Minox, Taba, Manavi, Segloes, Dannoni.' Internal evidence certainly suggests that *loca* here means more than any old place names, rather formal meeting places. Admittedly, Mixa, Panovius, and Minox have no identifiable associations with any geographical or societal features. The rest, however, could have specific links with southern Scotland.

Maponi can be connected with the Celtic hunter-god Maponus, worshipped in France in the territory of the Arverni in central France, and also known in northern Britain. The name has etymological links to Dumfriesshire in the form of Lochmaben and the Clochmabenstane, an ancient boulder on the shore of the Solway Firth which was a point of assembly in medieval times where international negotiations between the Scots and the English also took place. Megalithic boulders made suitably recognisable meeting places, and another one features as the Clack Mannan, the stone of the Celtic sea-god Manannán, or Manau. Manau was also the name of the district to the very north of the territory of the Votadini, incorporating the lands on the far side of the Forth on which Stirling and Clackmannan were later established, and Manau and Manavi are etymologically connected. Until comparatively recently, the waters of the Forth came right up to Clackmannan, in whose market place the

Clack Mannan still stands, bolted on top of a block of similar stone quarried in 1833 from the outcrop of rock nearby on which is the Wallace Monument.

Taba, if it is a copyist's error for Tava, is the Latin word for the river Tay — and B in the Cyrillic alphabet is the same as the English V. Segloes could be a further copyist's mistake, for Selgo[v]e[n]s[is], in Latin the adjectival form of Selgovae, while Dannoni could be regarded as too close to Damnonii to be coincidental. In these five names then, we have potential tribal meeting places for the Novantae, Selgovae, Damnonii, the northern Votadini, and beyond them, on the very limit between the protectorate and the northern tribes, the Venicones or their successors. The encouragement and exploitation of decentralised, local governments was the imperial policy of the Romans towards defeated or annexed peoples: centralisation suited them better when dealing with a territory from which they had withdrawn. What was now beginning to happen, however, was a change from tribal confederacy to the beginnings of a kingdom.

The formal peace imposed by Rome and accepted, as far as one can tell, by the southern tribes in Scotland, was in stark contrast to the cataclysmic changes which were in the meantime affecting the Roman empire at large.

Macrinus never made it to Rome. After 14 months of further campaigning in the east, he was defeated in a rebellion by his own troops, who then executed him. They resented the two-track system of army pay whereby recruits received less than veterans, which he had introduced as an economy measure after Caracalla's inflationary pay rises, and favoured as emperor Elagabalus, 14-year-old son of Julia Soaemias (c.185–222). She was a daughter of Julia Maesa (c.170–226), the sister of Severus's empress, and thus Elagabalus was Caracalla's first cousin once removed. Elagabalus, according to Cassius Dio a notoriously depraved transsexual, was, with his mother, brutally assassinated and dismembered four years later by the imperial guard. He was succeeded in 222 by his cousin Alexander Severus, 16-year-old son of Julia Mammaea (c.185–235), another daughter of Julia Maesa. Alexander ruled tolerably well for 13 years, since he was happy to take advice, especially from his mother. He took her on campaign with him to Germany, where in 235 they were caught up in an army mutiny and killed.

The revolt was instigated by Maximinus (c.173–238), a giant Thracian who was originally a shepherd and had risen through the ranks to become commander of the imperial guard. He proclaimed himself emperor, doubled army pay, and continued the military campaign. When the senate raised objections to his usurpation of power and nominated its own candidate, Maximinus invaded Italy in 238 and laid siege to Aquileia, where he was killed by his own troops. The chain reaction was a replay of the events of 69, several times over. Between 238 and 270 a further 25 emperors of Rome came and went, most of them violently. As the empire started to disintegrate, hostile peoples beyond its frontiers began to gather for the kill, among them the Alamanni, the Franks (a new threat), and the Goths in Germania, and the Parthians, who even managed to capture the emperor Valerian (c.195–260) in 259. He died a prisoner in their hands, leaving his son and co-emperor Gallienus (now about 35) to cope with trouble within the empire as well as pressures from outside it.

During the rule of Gallienus (253–68) so many military men in various parts of the empire proclaimed themselves emperor that they became known collectively as the 'thirty tyrants'. Some were put down by their own troops; all had to be dealt with. One of them actually got away with it for nine years. In 260, Gaius Licinius Postumus, Gallienus's commander on the Rhine front, assassinated one of Gallienus's sons and the commander of the imperial guard, who were in Cologne, and established a dominion of Gaul, with its own senate. Until he too was murdered by his own troops in 269, he not only managed, with the moral, military, and naval support of the Roman provinces of Britain, Spain, and Germany, to survive but also successfully to stave off determined efforts to overrun the empire by the hostile Germanic tribes, of whom the Franks had to be forcibly expelled from Gaul and Spain.

After Postumus's three successors had gone the same way in quick succession, the Gallic senate in 271 appointed as ruler one of their own number, Gaius Pius Tetricus. In the meantime, Gallienus had been assassinated; the plot to kill him involved several of his own officers, two of whom succeeded him in turn. Claudius II died in 270, it is said of the plague, having stoutly defended the empire against invasions and removed the Goths from serious contention for the next hundred years. The troops in Italy set up his brother as emperor, but then murdered him on hearing that the armies on the Danube frontier, where Claudius had been campaigning, had in 270 proclaimed his co-conspirator, Lucius Domitius Aurelianus (Aurelian), as emperor.

Aurelian (214/5–70), another fine soldier, strengthened the Danube frontier, and withdrew behind it the garrisons which had been in Dacia, only for the Alamanni to invade Italy for the fourth time. Aurelian took the opportunity at Ariminum to destroy that particular threat for good. He was, however, sufficient of a realist to order the city of Rome to be encircled by a great defensive wall, which was completed after his death. Built of concrete, with a facing of triangular bricks, it was about 12½ miles (20km) long, 13ft (4m) thick, and 24ft (7.2m) high.

The problem of the breakaway dominion of Gaul was resolved when Tetricus surrendered to Aurelian's army. Tetricus was made to walk in the procession celebrating Aurelian's triumph in 274, wearing Gallic trousers, a yellow tunic, and a scarlet cloak. Alongside him was Zenobia, regent for her two sons of the city of Palmyra, which had also revolted against Roman rule and had threatened to destabilise the eastern provinces. Aurelian, by masterly tactics, had marched his army across 120 miles (200km) of desert, and captured her. When he got to Thrace on his return march, he learned that supporters of Zenobia had massacred the garrison he had left in Palmyra. He turned his army about, took the rebels by surprise, and destroyed the city. Zenobia walked in the triumph bedecked with jewels and bound with golden chains, which attendants carried for her. Afterwards Aurelian granted her a generous pension and a house in Tivoli, and found Tetricus a good local government job in Lucania, where he lived into old age.

After five fruitful years in office, Aurelian was assassinated in 275 by members of his own staff. The usual dreadful chaos which ensued was only resolved nine years and 11 emperors later, when Valerius Diocletianus (Diocletian), a 39-year-old Dalmatian of obscure birth, emerged as ruler. The following year, 285, he split the empire for administrative purposes into two constituent parts, east and west, thus acknowledging the traditional cultural divide between them. Much of the region from Macedonia and Cyrenaica to the east was Greek, or had been Hellenised since the time of Alexander the Great (356–323 BC). Rome had received its initial culture from Greece, but had developed from that its own distinctive brand, which it imposed upon a society in the western empire which was largely Celtic. Diocletian appointed a Dalmatian colleague, Marcus Aurelius Valerius Maximianus (Maximian), about four years his junior, as deputy emperor (and in 286 co-emperor), in charge of Africa and the west. He himself retained responsibility for the east.

The repeated attempts to undermine the empire from within do not seem to have impinged upon the situation in Lower Britain. The next one, however, certainly did so. For some years the coastal regions on either side of the Channel had been subjected to fierce attacks by bands of Frank and Saxon pirates. Some 300 years before this, the senate had appointed Pompey the 'Great' to rid the Mediterranean of pirates, which, with the resources allocated to him, he comprehensively achieved in three months. Maximian assigned Marcus Mausaeus Carausius, an army man with experience as a youth of piloting river craft on his native Belgian coast, to the job of forcing this new threat out of business. The implication is that the existing fleets, probably controlled by the governors of Upper Britain and Lower Germany respectively, did not individually have the skills, the resources, and the training to cope with this continuing terrorist activity. They were more used to extensive periods of transport duties at sea and building assignments on land, interspersed with brief all-out actions using conventional methods of naval warfare. Their ships and men were not equipped to patrol the narrow seas in all weathers under oars, and then suddenly be called upon to engage smaller, more manoeuvrable boats, with sails as well as oars, handled by experienced seamen.

Carausius concentrated his combined, and augmented, fleets at his headquarters in Boulogne, where it is suggested that he employed a novel method of combating the pirates. Through his intelligence network he obtained prior knowledge of where the next attack would be, and allowed it to take place. He would then ambush the pirates on their way back to their base, and confiscate their booty, which he diverted to his personal treasury. It is said that when Maximian learned what was going on, he ordered the execution of Carausius, who took evasive action. Whether or not this version of events is true, there was certainly a great falling out between them, as a result of which in 286 Carausius, from his base still at Boulogne, declared himself emperor and set himself up as a breakaway ruler of Britain and part of northern Gaul.

The charisma, and chutzpah, of Carausius enabled him to survive for seven years, and his regime to last for ten. All three legions in Britain backed him, and as well as his existing naval command he obtained the support of individual units of nine legions stationed in the region of the Rhine. He established a mint in London, and another at Rouen, from which he issued several series of coins designed to cause as much embarrassment as possible to the establishment in Rome. He called himself Marcus Aurelius, and inscriptions on his coins referred to Diocletian, Maximian, and himself as the 'three Augustuses'. One depicted all three of them, with the caption 'Carausius and his brothers'; another, showing Carausius being welcomed by Britannia, is inscribed, 'Come, the one for whom we have waited', a literary allusion to Virgil's *Aeneid* (II. 283).

With all the available warships in the hands of Carausius, Maximian was forced to build a new fleet before he could begin to take any action against him. With this, he sailed down the Rhine in 289 and somehow broke out into the North Sea, only to be defeated by either Carausius or the weather, or both; the literary sources are not clear on this point. There even appears to have been some sort of tacit agreement that there would be no more hostilities. If so, it was broken in 292, the year Diocletian made a further reorganisation at the top. He and Maximian remained senior emperors, with the title of Augustus, while two new deputies were appointed, each with the title of Caesar: Galerius (*c.*250–311) and Flavius Valerius Constantius (*c.*250–306), who had acquired the surname Chlorus, the 'Pale'. Constantius was given authority over Britain, Gaul, and Spain, in which capacity in 293 he besieged Boulogne from the mainland, having blocked the entrance to the harbour with piles and rocks. The garrison surrendered, and Carausius, now without his continental base, was murdered by his chief finance officer, Allectus, who assumed the role of ruler of Britain.

Three years later, Constantius took on the rebels in Britain itself. His fleet sailed in two divisions, one commanded by himself, the other by Julius Asclepiodotus, commander of Constantius's imperial guard. Asclepiodotus got there first; Allectus was killed in battle and the regime collapsed. A fortuitous fog caused part of Constantius's division to divert to the port of London, which was on the point of being sacked by Frankish mercenaries from Allectus's army, bent on retrieving some reward for their services overseas before returning home. Eumenius (*c.*260–*c.*311), who was Constantius's secretary and a famous orator, delivered an address in 297 complimenting him on his victories, in which he describes the citizens of London being treated to a gladiatorial show as the Franks were slaughtered. Constantius arrived too late to take part in the show, but not too late to take the credit for it.

Allectus had effectively withdrawn the garrisons from Hadrian's Wall in order to fight Constantius, though in the event he did not put all his forces into the battle – this was probably due to the surprise tactics of the opposition. It is a reasonable assumption that the northern tribes took the opportunity of this absence to overrun the wall and create some havoc within the province of Britain, as they, and elements from Ireland and from the continent, had been doing for some years. Constantius stayed in Britain until the following year, restoring order within the province and instigating repair and building work in the vicinity of the wall. According to Eumenius's address, the northernmost tribes now obeyed his every wish. These, according to Eumenius, now include the Picts, the first known reference to any people of that name.

Diocletian further reorganised the administration of Italy and the provinces of the empire into 116 divisions, in 12 groups (*dioceses*), each controlled by a deputy (*vicarius*), answerable to one of the four commanders of the imperial guards. By 314, the diocese of Britain consisted of four provinces, with the diocesan headquarters being in London. In 305, Diocletian, having ruled the empire for 21 years, abdicated, and required Maximian to do the same. Constantius and Galerius now became joint-emperors, and two new Caesars were appointed: Maximinus (270–313), nephew and adopted son of Galerius, and Flavius Valerius Severus (d. 307), also a protégé of Galerius, to rule the west under Constantius. Diocletian, now in his sixties, retired to his palace in his native Dalmatia, where he died in 313. In the meantime he read philosophy and attended his garden, while stoutly refusing to involve himself in the now almost inevitable wrangles over the succession.

Constantius's first priority as emperor seems to have been to settle any outstanding problems in northern Britain. Already a sick man, he elected to take with him not Severus, but Constantine, his own son by his first wife. They crossed from Boulogne in 306, and if the words of a panegyric to Constantine of 310, possibly again written by Eumenius, are to be believed, a resounding military victory was achieved over the 'Caledonians and other Picts'. Immediately after this

Constantius died in York; an anonymous biography of Constantine, written in about 390, refers to his father dying 'after defeating the Picts' (*Excerpta Valesiani* 2. 4).

That there was a campaign against the northern tribes at this time need not be doubted. Whether its purpose was to drive them out of the vicinity of Hadrian's Wall, or even out of the northern regions of the province of Britain, back to their homelands, or whether Constantius actually took his forces into their territory, is open to question. Constantine's panegyrist suggests that Constantius, recognising the approach of death, vowed to reach the end of the world, as Septimius Severus had done, and Agricola before him. The brief account of this feat, however, echoes so closely Cassius Dio's description of Severus's last campaign, that it may have been intended simply as a literary, and metaphorical, parallel. There is, however, some slight archaeological evidence to support the invasion theory. Pottery from the early fourth century has been discovered at both Cramond and Carpow, though this could indicate no more than an exploratory expedition by sea. In 2003 a worn coin, dating from 268–70, was picked up in a field near a marching camp at Forteviot. Taken with the foregoing evidence, this might suggest a combined naval and military operation such as both Agricola and Severus had conducted.

On learning of the death of Constantius, Galerius very properly promoted Valerius Severus to the post of Augustus; the army in Britain had other ideas, and acclaimed Constantine as emperor. The ensuing bloodbath, involving at one point six men styling themselves Augustus, was not finally resolved until 324, when Constantine defeated, and later executed, the last of his rivals for supreme power, his brother-in-law Licinius. Constantine the 'Great', who ruled until 337, is regarded as the first Christian monarch, though he was not himself baptised until just before his death. He also made Byzantium the seat of government of Rome, renaming it Constantinople, and thus ensured that an eastern Roman empire of a kind was able to survive the eventual loss of the west.

Meanwhile, the province of Britain itself was undergoing a growth in economic prosperity. There was little unrest within the province itself. The military were primarily concerned with guarding the official postal system and consignments of money and precious metals, and on occasions with supervising the collection of taxes. The east and south-east coastal defences were strengthened against the Frankish raiders. Behind Hadrian's Wall each principal fort had its unwalled *vicus*, a bustling centre of activity and trade covering an area of up to 12 acres (5ha) or more. It is true that towns which had now become predominantly civilian localities were being provided with walls, but these were to protect citizens from lawless elements within the community, not from barbarian invaders. Unlike Gaul, however, where town walls often enclosed only the area containing public buildings, walls in Britain encircled much of the existing extent of the town, suggesting generous municipal treasury grants. There are signs, too, that as late as the end of the fourth century AD, rebuilding work was being undertaken in towns such as St Albans, an indication of an urban community flourishing at a time of particular unrest. In the country, increased production, for military and civilian consumption at home and for supply to the troops on the continent, is reflected in the number of luxurious villas which date from the fourth century. To Britain too came wealthy landowners from Gaul, refugees from the uncertainties of living near the Rhine frontier.

In the lightly forested area to the immediate south of Hadrian's Wall, there were numerous circular or rectangular farmsteads, often with their own field systems. Hardly any of them had defensive ditches. Here there was a predominance of arable farming, for which the garrisons on the wall and their attendant settlements provided a ready market. In the corresponding area to the north of the wall, sites were more scattered. About one-fifth of these were defended by multiple ditch systems, and none had fields associated with them. Grassland predominated, suggesting that stock farming was more significant than the raising of crops.

Of the Celtic tribes in southern Scotland, the Votadini certainly survived into the dark ages which overtook Britain after the final Roman retreat, and maybe the Novantae and Selgovae too. Farther north, the overruling influence was wielded now by the Picts. The name *Picti* means in Latin 'painted people', or, as has been suggested, 'tattooed people'. We do not know what they called themselves. The Greek navigator and astronomer Pytheas, who sailed along the east coast of Britain in 325 BC, named the land the Pretanic Isles, from Pretani, or Pritani, a name for the inhabitants of those islands. That name came to be associated specifically with those in the south of Britain, with the variant

ORKNEY

Caithness

ATTACOTTI

Birnie

Mounth

PICTS

ARGYLL

Forteviot

Firth of Tay

Carpow

MANAU

FIFE

Clackmannan

Firth of Forth

Falkirk

Cramond

VOTADINI

Traprain Law

DAMNONII

Cappuck

High Rochester

SELGOVAE

Risingham

NOVANTAE

Lochmaben

Birrens

Netherby

Bewcastle

HADRIAN'S WALL

Solway Firth

NORTHUMBRIA

14 Scotland, third and fourth centuries AD, with places mentioned in chapter 8

Priteni applying to those in the north. In all its forms, as does the Old Irish version Cruithni, describing Picts who settled in Ireland, it means 'people of the designs'. And from Pritani came the Latin form Britannia, for the province, and Britanni for its people, who called themselves Brittones. In the northern territory outside the province, the terms Priteni and Picti became synonymous.

For the Picts to be cited by Eumenius in AD 297, it follows that they must have existed before then. The phrase of 310, 'Caledonians and other Picts', suggests a regrouping, and perhaps also renaming, of the indigenous Celtic tribes north of the Clyde–Forth isthmus. Ammianus Marcellinus (c.330–95) wrote in Latin in about 390 a continuation of the histories of Tacitus, of which we have 17 books out of the original 31, covering the years AD 353–78. For the year 368, he describes the Picts as being 'divided into two tribes, Dicaledonians and Verturiones' (*Res Gestae* XXVII.8.5), who may simply represent the older Caledonians and Maeatae. The significance of the emergence of the Picts is that they represented an independent and recognisable society and culture which survived until about AD 900, well into the Christian era in Scotland. The dual tribal confederacy, however, seems to have been maintained. Irish annals describe Dubthalorc, who died in 782, as 'king of the Picts this side of the Mounth', that is a line drawn across the country from the natural barrier to the south-west of Aberdeen.

The Picts left no documentary sources of their own. We have, however, references to their mythical origins, traditions, and history in the works of Irish and English annalists, and in the *Pictish Chronicle* (also known as the *Old Scottish Chronicle*), a tenth-century manuscript preserved in a fourteenth-century copy. They left, too, evidence of their distinctive artwork in the form of carvings on stone. Examples of delicately worked geometric symbols, representations of animals, birds, and fish, and bold human figures, incised on undressed stones, and designs carved in relief on dressed stones have been discovered in Shetland and Orkney, and from Caithness to the Tay. We know, from personal and place names, the Gallo-Brittonic dialect that they probably spoke. We also have, preserved in a handful of short memorial inscriptions, an insight into a Pictish 20-letter alphabet, known as ogam, which originated in Ireland in about AD 300. The letters comprise one to four horizontal or diagonal strokes or lines, incised to the left or right, or across, a vertical line, which was often the natural break or angle between the planes or faces of the rock from which the stone was made. They were read upwards, from the bottom of the inscription.

It has been observed from two lists of Pictish kings, believed to date from the tenth century, that for the historical period from about AD 200 to 780, no son succeeded his father. This, with the fact that the fathers of two seventh-century Pictish kings were not themselves from Pictland, has been taken as confirmation of the validity of an Irish legend recorded by Bede (c.673–735), the Northumbrian cleric and historian, who wrote in Latin:

> It is said that some Picts from [Scandinavia] put to sea in a few longships, and were driven by storms around the coasts of Britain, arriving at length on the north coast of Ireland. Here they found the nation of the Scots [i.e. Irish Dál Riata], from whom they asked permission to settle. . . . The Scots replied that there was not room for them both, but said: 'We can give you good advice. We know that there is another island not far to the east, which we often see in the distance on clear days. If you choose to go there, you can make it fit to live in; should you meet resistance, we will come to your help.' So the Picts crossed into Britain, and began to settle in the north of the island, since the Britons were in possession of the south. Having no women with them, these Picts asked wives of the Scots, who consented on condition that, when any dispute arose, they should choose a king from the female royal line rather than the male. This custom continues among the Picts to this day.
>
> *A History of the English Church and People,*
> tr. Leo Shirley Price, rev. R. E. Latham, I. 1

In other words, in such circumstances a king could be succeeded by a son of his sister, or of his daughter, but not by his own son. This principle of matrilinear succession would make the Picts unique among the Celtic tribes in Britain.

An alternative view, however, now tends to prevail. One of the foundation myths of the Picts tells of the seven sons of Cruithne, each of whom ruled a part of Pictland, from Caithness to Fife. This system of seven tribal kings under an overlord recurs among the Celts in Ireland. Out of this comes the suggestion that each of the kings in the king lists was an overlord, ruling the whole of Pictland or the north or south tribal confederacy, and that this office rotated among the tribal kings. Thus even in a society in which the life of a king was short as well as brutal, his son would be most unlikely still to be living when the turn of his tribe came round again. The two non-Pictish overlords are seen as puppet kings, temporarily imposed on the Picts by more powerful neighbours to the south. It has also been stressed that Bede says that matrilineage was to be applied only 'when a dispute arose', and not necessarily as a general practice. His story, indeed, and the Irish legend on which it is based, have been explained as Irish propaganda, devised at a time when the Dál Riata had designs on Pictland.

In such a society survival depends on arms and the ability to wield them skilfully. That the Picts were formidable fighters to survive so long would go without saying, were it not also for the evidence of literary sources and the depictions of warriors and battles on their stones. They were, too, a seafaring race, capable of deploying a large fleet anywhere between the Orkneys and the Northumbrian shore. Their fighting capabilities, therefore, on land and at sea were a match for anything but the most enthusiastic, battle-hardened Roman forces.

After the death of Constantine in 337, his three sons became joint emperors. In 340 Flavius Julius Constans (c.321–50), the third and youngest son, resisted an attempt by his eldest brother Constantine II (b. 316) to usurp some of his imperial territories, and killed him in battle. He now appropriated for himself the provinces for which Constantine had had responsibility since the death of their father: Britain, Gaul, and Spain. In 343 something happened sufficiently serious to bring Constans to Britain in January, the worst month for weather in those parts. The book in which Ammianus describes this expedition is lost. The operation may, however, have been connected with the fact that archaeological evidence indicates that the outpost forts of Risingham, High Rochester, and Bewcastle, and also possibly Netherby, were destroyed at some point during the first half of the fourth century, and High Rochester, the farthest north of them, was not rebuilt.

From a cross-reference, though, in Ammianus, it is possible to identify an administrative change made by Constans to improve the gathering of information about the activities of the tribes north of Hadrian's Wall. The *exploratores* were replaced by a force called *arcani* or *areani*, depending on which reading one prefers – neither appears elsewhere in this form. An ingenious case has been made for *areani*, that it is associated with the word that means 'sheepfold', and reflects the kind of accommodation which might have been provided for these operatives. *Arcani*, on the other hand, can readily be associated with the adjective *arcanus*, meaning 'secret' or 'private' (English, arcane), and thus would refer to a force of spies or secret agents. Ammianus says: 'Their function was to disperse widely, near and far, and obtain information for the army command of any unrest between neighbouring tribes' (*Res Gestae* XXVIII. 3. 8).

There was trouble within the province of Britain in 353. In a palace revolution in 350, Magnentius, the grandson of one of the Germanic settlers introduced by Constantine into the empire to bolster his armies, replaced Constans, who was then murdered. Magnentius, who had a British father, was defeated in Pannonia in 351 by Constantius II (317–61), second son of Constantine, and lived on for another two years before killing himself. His death was the signal for reprisals against his supporters in Britain, and against those who, with his encouragement, had embraced pagan ways of worship in a society which was now officially Christian. These were organised by Constantius's imperial notary, Paulus, whose overenthusiastic investigative policy earned him the sobriquet *Catena*, the 'Chain'. His accusations, and his tactics in trying to make them stick, became so outrageous that the *vicarius* of Britain, Flavius Martinus, threatened to resign if those who were obviously innocent were not released. Instead, Martinus was forced to commit suicide.

This reign of terror was one in a series of distressing incidents which affected morale in the province of Britain, as Ammianus records for the year 360. It also appears that in the meantime, outside the province itself, some sort of treaty had again been engineered with the tribes in the far north:

> Eruptions by the savage tribes, the Scots and the Picts, who had broken the peace agreement, were causing havoc in the regions around the frontier and instilling fear into the people of the province, who were worn out by the catalogue of past disasters.
>
> *Res Gestae* XX. 1. 1.

So we now find the Picts in some kind of alliance with the Dál Riata, to whom Latin writers referred as *Scotti* or *Scoti*, an Irish word which means 'bandits' or 'pirates'. Only after about 900 is it strictly appropriate to use the term 'Scot' to describe a denizen of Scotland; before that it means a descendant of the Celtic Dál Riata, from north-east Ireland, who began to settle in Argyll in about 500, and who spoke a form of Old Irish which became Scottish Gaelic and replaced Pictish.

The attacks on Hadrian's Wall and its environs were intensified in 364, which was marked by renewed unrest on the frontiers of the empire:

> Now, as though the trumpets were blowing for war throughout the whole Roman world, the most fearsome tribes mobilised and poured across the nearest frontiers. At one and the same time, the Alamanni were causing havoc in Gaul and Raetia, and the Sarmatae and Quadi in Pannonia; while Picts, Saxons, Scots, and Attacotti were inflicting on the Britons a continuous series of calamities. The Austoriani and other Mauretanian tribes erupted into Africa more violently than ever before, and predatory hordes of Goths looted Thrace. The king of Persia forcefully seized Armenia, eager to call it his property once more.
>
> Ammianus Marcellinus, *Res Gestae* XXVI. 4. 5–6

The stage was set for the ultimate gesture of defiance by the northern tribes of Britain.

9

TOWARDS A NATION

Constantius II died in 361 while on the way to silence his deputy-emperor, Julian, whose troops had acclaimed him Augustus. To give Constantius his due, however, it is said that on his deathbed he nominated Julian as his successor.

Flavius Claudius Julianus (331–63) was, on his father's side, a first cousin of Constantius, who had in 355 appointed him Caesar with responsibility for the western empire. Julian, a hands-on administrator as well as a military man, built 400 new ships in 359 to augment his transport fleet which regularly brought grain from Britain to the armies on the Rhine, though at what cost to the Britons is not recorded. In 360, he decided that he was too preoccupied with the Alamanni to deal personally with whatever problems were brewing on his north-west frontier. Instead, he sent his commander-in-chief, Lupicinus, with four companies of light-armed auxiliaries, to cross from Boulogne in dead of winter, and to clear up the situation by force or by diplomacy. It is probable that Lupicinus got no farther than London before being recalled when the political map changed.

As emperor, Julian was known as the 'Apostate': he reacted against his Christian upbringing and, as is the nature of converts, applied a fanatical intensity to the self-imposed task of restoring pagan worship throughout the empire. He was the last non-Christian emperor, as well as the last of the house of Constantine. He died in 363 after being speared in the belly by a Persian guerilla while retreating from an eastern campaign. He was briefly succeeded by Jovian (331–64), who died in Bithynia of what has been variously recorded as overeating, poisonous (or poisoned) mushrooms, or asphyxiation by fumes from a charcoal fire or a freshly painted bedroom. A convention of civilian and military officials, hastily arranged at Nicaea, nominated as emperor

Valentinian I (321–75), on condition that he appoint a co-emperor. When he chose his brother Valens (c.328–78) as ruler in the east, no-one dared raise any objection.

Valentinian was primarily a military man, one of the last of the true warrior-emperors. His reactions to the events in Britain of 364 are not recorded. What happened next, he could not ignore.

Ammianus Marcellinus, from whom the information comes, was a professional soldier of about 34 at the time, and had served on both eastern and western fronts. As a historian, he had a philosophical turn of mind and an awareness of the significance of the truth. And when he published his account of the momentous events of 367, there would have been people still alive who experienced them at first hand.

> Valentinian [on his way to fight the Alamanni] was much disturbed by alarming reports which indicated that Britain had been paralysed by a barbarian conspiracy; Nectaridus, commander of the [eastern] coastal regions, had been killed, and a senior military officer, Fullofaudes, had been ambushed and captured by the enemy. . . . The Picts, as well as the Attacotti, a race of warlike men, and the Scots, were ranging far and wide and causing much devastation; while Franks, Saxons, and neighbouring peoples, wherever they could burst in by land or sea, were laying waste the shores of Gaul, looting, burning, and murdering all their prisoners.
>
> *Res Gestae* XXVII. 8. 1/5

The Attacotti, whom St Jerome (c.342–420) claims to have observed in Gaul eating human flesh with every enjoyment, have been associated with the Western Isles. The damage to buildings, military installations, and social infrastructure caused by this combined, and totally unexpected, operation was catastrophic. The mere notion of a simultaneous land and sea attack by peoples of different cultural backgrounds was unprecedented. Military morale in Britain, however, was low. Pay chests were being intercepted in transit and their contents hijacked by senior officers. Discharges or exemptions from duty were openly sold. Soldiers, deprived of their means of subsistence, were deserting in droves. Moreover, the *arcani*, according to Ammianus, had been bribed 'at different times, by the promise or receipt of considerable loot, to pass on to the barbarians intelligence about what was going on among our troops' (*Res Gestae* XXVIII. 3. 8).

The nature of that intelligence was sound. The deal with the *arcani* almost certainly bound them not to give any warning of attack, and the secrecy with which the operation was mounted and the tactical ferocity with which it was undertaken were impeccable. There are, perhaps unsurprisingly, no accounts of the actual assaults on the province of Britain by the Picts and Scots and Attacotti, only of the measures to restore order after they had occurred. It would seem, however, that the Picts swarmed across the wall, which to be fair was not intended on its own to be a defence against concerted attacks, causing serious damage to the structure. They sacked and burned the forts and the settlements that had grown up around them. Then, bypassing the legionary fortresses, they penetrated farther south, perhaps even as far as London. Their ships, sailing along the east coast, could have provided support while increasing the general chaos on land by making lightning raids on towns and military installations. The *classis Britannica* was either overwhelmed or failed to arrive in time.

The Scots and Attacotti probably concentrated on the western coast, as far as the Severn estuary, landing military units almost at will. Army deserters and runaway slaves joined the permanent gangs of bandits in terrorising law-abiding citizens in rural areas. All the while, the Franks and Saxons concentrated their attacks on northern Gaul, but they may also have landed raiding parties on the east and south-east coasts of Britain.

It was not within the Celtic temperament to acquire territory other than to meet the call for extra accommodation. Having effectively overrun the province of Britain, for whose lands they apparently had no need, the invaders from the north settled instead for plunder in the form of slaves, cattle, and removable items of value. Yet such was the rule of chaos created by their depredations, that the first two military commanders sent by Valentinian to deal with the situation each returned without having achieved anything tangible.

Valentinian now gave the British command to Theodosius, called the 'elder' to distinguish him from his son, Theodosius I (emperor 379–95), who accompanied his father on this expedition. In the spring of 368 they crossed from Boulogne to Richborough, where they awaited the arrival of the four companies of auxiliary infantry which had been allocated to them. Then they marched to London, where Theodosius set up his headquarters.

He divided his troops into small units, which tore into the bands of hostile marauders who were ranging over the countryside weighed down
by sacks of loot, and speedily put to flight those who were driving along
prisoners and cattle. They confiscated the booty of which the poor tax-
payers had been deprived; this Theodosius returned to its owners, less a
small commission for his exhausted soldiers.

Ammianus Marcellinus, *Res Gestae* XXVII. 8. 8

Theodosius then offered an amnesty to army deserters and those
who had overstayed their leave, which most of them gratefully accepted. He removed the *arcani* from their positions. He reorganised the
administration structure of the province, and asked for two men of
strong character and proven ability to be sent to head up the civil and
military arms of the operation. It is to be presumed that those who had
invaded the province so peremptorily were killed, imprisoned, or sent
on their way back to their homelands. The next year he would tackle
the problem of how to keep them there.

In the meantime he had to deal with an unwanted and unwarrant-
ed complication. Twenty years earlier, some coins had been minted and
circulated in Britain carrying the name of Carausius II, about whom
nothing else is known. Now, there was yet another revolt in the
province against the empire. It was instigated by Valentinus, a Roman
citizen from Pannonia, who had been exiled to Britain for some crime
which Valentinian decided did not qualify for the death sentence. Maybe
this had something to do with the fact that Valentinus's brother-in-law,
Maximinus, had insinuated himself into the favour of the emperor, who
also came from Pannonia and was a staunch Christian, by energetically
prosecuting in the courts members of the Roman aristocracy whom he
believed guilty of performing magic. Theodosius, however, had been
having Valentinus watched, and was able to scotch his designs, though
there is in Ammianus more than a suggestion that Theodosius was
aware, too, of other potential uprisings in the province.

It was dangers from within the province, as much as further invasions
from outside, that led Theodosius to strengthen town defences as well
as to restore structural damage to buildings. This he did so effectively
that when the evacuation began of serving units needed to bolster
imperial support on the mainland, such towns were able successfully to
survive well into the fifth century.

For a man of method and application, Theodosius's restoration of Hadrian's Wall gives evidence that it was a botched and hasty job, maybe undertaken by local forced labour rather than professional craftsmen. The masonry is crude, with unsuitable stone being employed. Perforce, civilian settlements were merged with the forts, and orderly arrangements of custom-built structures gave way to huddled communities in which the military shared their accommodation with their families and with other civilians, including children.

North of the wall, the last outpost forts, Netherby, Bewcastle, and Risingham, were finally abandoned. The troops garrisoning the wall itself were now the forward defence of the frontier. The *arcani* were not replaced. Instead, a stronger relationship was forged with some of the lowland tribes. Among these were almost certainly the Novantae and Votadini, who may, in return for bribes and promises of protection, have enjoyed the status of client kingdoms, charged with defending the province of Britain against raids from the north. Cunnedda, the celebrated chief of the Votadini of Manau, who, in the second quarter of the fifth century, led his people in a mass migration to north Wales, is recorded as having a grandfather, Padarn, whose surname, *pes-rut*, means 'scarlet cloak'. This is taken to be a symbol of authority conferred by the Romans, equating to the rank of auxiliary commander.

The contemporary panegyrist Claudian (*c*.370–*c*.404), who wrote in Latin verse, has some colourful references to naval operations in the north which he claims were undertaken by Theodosius at this time: none more so than the Orkneys being crammed with Saxon dead, the Shetlands drenched with blood of Picts, and Hibernia [Ireland] weeping for piles of Scots' dead. That there was some action of this kind would appear to be attested by the *Notitia Dignitatum*, an early fifth-century inventory of military establishments and units, which lists four companies of Attacotti as having been recruited to, or forcibly enlisted in, the Roman army.

On his return to Rome in 369, Theodosius was promoted to *magister equitum*, commander-in-chief of the cavalry, a post originating in 509 BC, when a dictator (who held power for only six months) was empowered to nominate his own appointee with that title as his deputy. Theodosius remained in that position until 375, when Valentinian had him executed. Valentinian himself died later that year, it is said from an apoplectic stroke brought on by the attitude of ambassadors from the

Quadi, who claimed that their chiefs were not responsible for acts committed by individual groups of terrorists living within their boundaries, an excuse with twenty-first-century echoes. He was succeeded as western emperor by his son Gratian (359–83). The eastern empire suffered a crushing defeat at Hadrianople in 378 at the hands of the Visigoths (Wise Goths), in the course of which Valens disappeared, presumed killed. In the wake of this disaster, Gratian appointed the younger Theodosius, now 32, as co-emperor in the east.

In 382, the Picts and Scots again made trouble of one kind or another, but were heavily defeated by Magnus Maximus, who had served with the elder Theodosius in Britain and was now commander of the Roman army in the province. Magnus reappears in the Welsh saga stories of *The Mabinogion* as Macsen Wledig (*wledig* or *gwledig* means ruler). He was also instrumental in founding a dynasty in Galloway (former territory of the Novantae), whose first ruler, with the Roman name Antonius, is recorded as having been descended from him.

Magnus overreached himself in 383. He withdrew some of the garrisons in Britain and crossed to Gaul as a potential Augustus, in which capacity he fought, and managed to kill, Gratian. He reached some agreement with Theodosius I, whereby they should each retain what territories they had, and that Valentinian II (371–92), son of Valentinian I by his second wife, should rule in Italy. In 387 Magnus invaded Italy, but was finally defeated, and executed, by Theodosius in 388. His widow, Elen Luyddog (St Helen of Caernarvon), was the daughter of a Celtic chieftain in Britain who ruled from Segontium, near Caernarvon. While with Magnus in Gaul, she had been converted to Christianity by Bishop (St) Martin of Tours (316–97). After Magnus's death, she returned to Wales, where she worked for the Church and initiated the building of roads to facilitate connections between tribes – some sections of roads which were originally Roman are still called Elen's highway. Of her numerous sons, Leo became king of the Cantiaci, Owain was said to be the ancestor of the rulers of Glywsing in south Wales, Demetus founded the dynasty that ruled Dyfed, and Antonius the dynasty that produced kings of the Isle of Man.

With no Magnus, and his legions, to oppose them, the Picts and Scots continued their raids. The not wholly reliable British historian Gildas (*c.*504–70) has a reference at this point to the construction of a turf wall right across the territory from sea to sea, which could be interpreted as an attempt to re-establish the Clyde–Forth line. Theodosius died in 395, and his able general Flavius Stilicho (*c*.359–408), the son of a Vandal captain, took up the campaign in his capacity also as guardian of Honorius (384–423), emperor in the west while his elder brother Arcadius (377/8–408) ruled the east. To judge from Claudian, writing of the year 400, he had some success:

> Then spoke Britannia, wrapped in the hide of some strange Caledonian beast, with her cheeks tattooed, and her sky-blue mantle sweeping over her footprints like the ocean's swell over the shore: 'Stilicho defended me when I, too, was about to be destroyed by peoples across the frontier, and the Scots stirred up all Hibernia, and the sea foamed with the pull of hostile oars. Thanks to his attentions, I would not fear the spears and javelins of the Scots, nor quake before the Picts, nor keep lookout along all my coastline at every changing wind for the coming of the Saxons.'
>
> *De Consulato Stilichonis* II. 247–55

A further mention by Gildas of a wall, this time of stone, could suggest that Stilicho pulled his frontier troops back to Hadrian's Wall. In 401, however, he was forced to withdraw forces from Britain to meet a threat not just against the empire, but against the city of Rome itself. The inexorable movement of peoples, which had begun some years earlier when the nomadic Huns broke out of their homelands on the plains of central Russia and surged westwards, had caused equally destructive migrations by the massed tribes in their way. Now the Visigoths, under their ruler Alaric (*c*.370–410), who was a canny negotiator as well as a warrior, were invading Italy.

According to Claudian, the troops withdrawn from Britain included the 'legion stationed to guard against those in the farthest north, which curbs the savage Scots, and observes the lifeless tattoos on the bodies of dying Picts' (*De Bello Gothico* 416–8). Gildas, if it is to this event that he is referring, graphically describes what happened next: 'No sooner were they gone, than the Picts and Scots, like worms which in the heat of mid-day come forth from their holes, hastily land again from their canoes. . . differing one from another in manners, but inspired with the same avidity for blood, and all the more eager to shroud their villainous faces in bushy hair than to cover with decent clothing those parts of their body which required it' (tr. J. A. Giles, *De Excidio et Conquestu Britanniae* 19, courtesy Internet Medieval Sourcebook).

In a series of battles in northern Italy in 402 and 403, Stilicho saw off the immediate danger from the Visigoths, but allowed Alaric simply to retreat to his new homeland in what is now Romania. The former British garrisons could not be returned; they were needed by Stilicho to fight off another threat, from the Ostrogoths (Bright Goths), now occupying the plains of Hungary.

Not only the Dál Riata were raiding from across the Irish Sea. Irish historical records, which begin about this time, tell of Niall Noígiallach (Niall of the Nine Hostages), who ruled in Tara. His mother is believed to have been a British princess carried off by his father during a raid. In about 405 he was pillaging the coasts of Britain and, as his name implies, presumably kidnapping members of wealthy families for ransom, and others as slaves. Such a slave was St Patrick (*c*.385–*c*.481), son of a Romanised Briton who was civic official and a deacon of the Christian Church. According to Patrick's own account, when he was 16 he was captured by Irish raiders from his home on the west coast somewhere in the vicinity of Hadrian's Wall. Hoards of loot from Britain in the form of late Roman silver hacked up into pieces and crushed flat, and silver coins, have been discovered in County Waterford and County Derry. A similar hoard, including church plate, was found at Traprain Law between 1914 and 1923. With the treasure were four silver coins, one of Valens and three of Arcadius and Honorius, suggesting a date of burial between 410 and 425. It could be loot brought back from the other side of Hadrian's Wall, or it could be payment to mercenary troops, or to local tribesmen helping to defend Britain against Picts, Scots, and Saxons.

In 406, with Stilicho pre-occupied on the eastern frontiers of continental Europe, what remained of the troops in Britain put up as emperor first Marcus, whom they soon murdered, and then Gratian, a local civilian administrator, who met the same fate in 407. He was replaced as emperor-elect by Constantine III (d. 411), who was a soldier, and had the right name for the job.

In the meantime, on the last day of 406, hordes of Alans, Suevi, and Vandals poured across the frozen Rhine and occupied northern Gaul. Some of them even reached the Pyrenees. Constantine, with what troops he could raise in Britain and on the continent, managed, by good

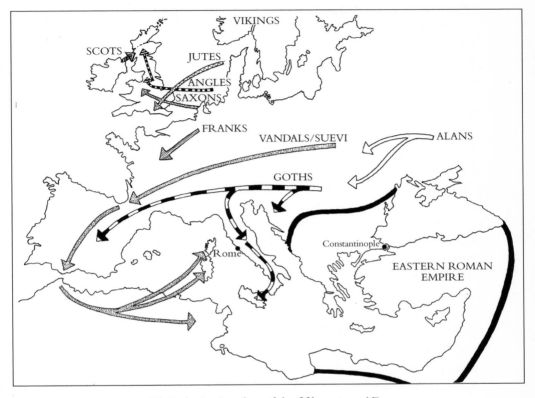

15 Barbarian invaders of the fifth century AD

generalship, to restore order in Gaul and also to defeat an army sent against him by Honorius. In May 408 he made Arles, in southern Gaul, his permanent headquarters.

In the same month of May 408, Arcadius died at the age of 31; the cause is unknown. He was succeeded, as he had intended, by his seven-year-old son, Theodosius II (401–50), under the guardianship of the Persian king, Isdigerdes (d. 421). Affairs of state were conducted by Anthemius, Arcadius's commander of the imperial guard, after whose death in 414 the role was undertaken by Theodosius's elder sister, (St) Pulcheria (399–453).

The death of Arcadius resolved a certain amount of friction between east and west, in the course of which Honorius, a notorious political ditherer, though to be fair he was now still only in his early twenties, had been persuaded to connive with Alaric to help him assert his claims to Illyricum. Alaric now demanded massive compensation in gold for his expenses in mounting the campaign, which Stilicho persuaded the senate to pay. Three months later, however, a conspiracy against Stilicho succeeded, and he was executed on the orders of Honorius.

In September Alaric and his army appeared before the walls of Rome and began a siege. He was persuaded to go away, after agreeing to accept from the famine-struck citizens more gold, numerous garments of silk and leather, and 3,000 pounds of pepper. He returned, however, in 409, and again in 410, when on 24 August someone opened the gates to him, and for three days his men sacked the city and burned buildings. When he left, he took with him Honorius's 20-year-old half-sister, Galla Placidia, later the wife of Constantius III (d. 421) and the mother of Valentinian III (419–55). Alaric died the following year, and was succeeded as leader of the Visigoths by his brother-in-law, Ataulf, who was murdered in 415 after a brief marriage with Placidia.

In 409, in the wake of a series of particularly damaging Saxon assaults, the various local authorities in the province of Britain, concluding that in the growing crisis it was better to organise their own defence than have it administered for them from a Mediterranean base, had replaced Constantine's officials with their own nominees. They informed Honorius of the actions they had taken to protect his, and their, interests and asked for his help. Honorius, who in the meantime had realised that he had little alternative other than to recognise Constantine as co-emperor in the west, replied in 410 that he could be of no practical assistance and that they should now fend for themselves.

The Roman empire in the west survived shakily until 476, when Odoacer (435–93), commander of the Roman army in Italy and chief of the German tribes that supplied most of the mercenaries of which it now consisted, deposed the 14-year-old emperor, Romulus Augustulus (d. *c*.?510), after he had ruled for ten months. The senate now despatched a deputation to Zeno (d. 491), emperor in the east, handing over to him the imperial insignia and asking him to recognise Odoacer as ruler in Italy. The empire in the east, which was not so vulnerable to attack from outside and enjoyed greater internal political stability, survived until 1453, when Constantinople fell to the Turks and the forces of Islam. In the meantime, in 1053, the Roman Catholic and Orthodox churches had gone their own doctrinal ways.

By the beginning of the fifth century AD, the Roman province of Britain had become an integral part of the Catholic Church. Caracalla's edict in 211 made all free inhabitants of Britain Roman citizens; they became also officially Christian in 391/2 under edicts of Theodosius I banning all pagan worship, including practices of the ancient Roman religion. The martyrdom of St Alban, graphically described by Bede, took place during a period of imperial persecution in either 208/9 or 301. Britain sent three bishops to Constantine's council at Arles in 314. That early Christianity in Britain as a whole was not purely an urban phenomenon is attested by inscriptions and finds of small items relating to Christianity, and also by place names. The late Latin term *ecclesia*, whose proper meaning is 'gathering' or 'assembly' (of Christians), survives in the many manifestations of Eccles and compounds, such as in Scotland Ecclefechan and Ecclesmachen.

The indispensable Bede has the earliest reference to Christianity in Scotland:

> The southern Picts, who live on this side of the mountains, are said to have abandoned the errors of idolatry long before [565] and accepted the true Faith through the preaching of Bishop Ninian, a most reverend and holy man of British race, who had been regularly instructed in the mysteries of the Christian Faith in Rome. Ninian's own episcopal see [is] named after St Martin and famous for its stately church. . .

The place. . . is commonly known as *Candida Casa*, the White House, because he built a church of stone, which was unusual among the Britons.

A History of the English Church and People,
tr. Leo Sherley-Price, rev. R. E. Latham, III. 4

The Scottish winter term-day Martinmas is called after St Martin. White House, translated into Old English, is Whithorn, in Galloway. It has recently been suggested that the inscribed slab of local stone, 4ft 4in (1.3m) high, discovered in the 1880s within the medieval priory complex and dating from 420–50, is in fact a building stone from the original church, and that the Latin inscription may refer to St Ninian himself. Among his disciples was Plebig, son of Magnus Maximus and Elen Luyddog.

The Picts were causing trouble in 429, when they, and a considerable force of Saxons, penetrated deep into central Britain, but were routed by St Germanus (*c.*378–448), then bishop of Auxerre, a cleric of remarkable all-round ability. Germanus was in Britain to counter the claims of a Christian group who professed themselves followers of the fifth-century heretic Pelagius. Having effectively defeated the Pelagian cause in a series of disputations at St Albans, Germanus, who was a former Roman army general, was persuaded to tackle the Picts and Saxons. This he did by first baptising his troops, and then ordering them to shout 'Alleluia!' as they went into the attack. Apparently, this so successfully rattled the opposition that they fled.

The Picts, however, soon regrouped, and now with the Scots renewed their campaigns of violence. For the Saxons, there was a new role, involving the shadowy figure of Vortigern (*c.*370–*c.*450). The eighth-century historian Nennius wrote a history of Britain in Latin, with access to fifth-century sources which are now lost: 'Vortigern ruled in Britain, and while he was ruler he was exercised by anxiety over the Picts and Scots, and further over a Roman attack, and not least by fear of Ambrosius' (*Historia Brittonum* 31). From this we may reasonably infer that there were at this time in Britain several regional rulers. Vortigern, who was married to Sevira, daughter of Magnus Maximus and Elen, was one, and Ambrosius another – Nennius also refers to a battle between Ambrosius and Vitalinus (whom some suggest might have been Vortigern himself, or at least an associate of his), probably in Hampshire, which has been dated to about 437.

For an insight into a potential 'Roman attack', we can refer to Gildas:

> Again, therefore, the wretched remnant, sending to Aetius, a powerful
> Roman citizen, address him as follows: 'To Aetius, now consul for the
> third time: the groans of the Britons. . . . The barbarians drive us to the
> sea; the sea throws us back on the barbarians: thus two modes of death
> await us, we are either slain or drowned.'
>
> *De Excidio et Conquestu Britanniae* 20,
> tr. J. A. Giles, courtesy Internet Medieval Sourcebook

The 'barbarians' were Saxon mercenaries whom Vortigern had introduced to Britain in about 430 to fight the Picts in return for land settlements in the south-east. Flavius Aetius (*c.*396–454), who knew the
cultures of the Visigoths and the Huns from being a hostage of both
when he was young, was military commander of the western empire, in
which capacity in 451 he was to inflict on Attila the Hun (*c.*406–53) the
only defeat in his lifetime. Aetius was consul four times, the third occasion in 446. By then, the Saxon settlers in Britain were well on their
way effectively to taking over the territory, and Aetius was too preoccupied in Gaul and Italy to mount an expedition to recover Britain for
Rome from Vortigern and his unwelcome allies.

As the Dark Ages dawned in Britain, Angles and Jutes joined the
flood of immigrants hostile to the now sub-Roman Britons. In the far
north-west a more peaceful incursion was taking place, as from around
450 members of the Dál Riata began to negotiate the 25-mile (40km)
sea journey to Argyll, not as armed allies, but as comparatively friendly
settlers in an antagonistic environment. Any uneasy alliance did not last,
however, for in 559 they were defeated and subdued by Brude
MacMaelchon, king of the Picts. Other upheavals were taking place. By
about the middle of the sixth century the Votadini had evolved into the
people of Gododdin, ruled from Din Eidyn (Edinburgh). South of the
Gododdin was the Anglian kingdom of Bernicia, with its coastal fortress
of Bamburgh. The British kingdoms of Strathclyde and, to the south,
Rheged, occupied the territories which had previously belonged to the
Damnonii, Novantae, and Selgovae.

In about 565, Brude, in his castle near Inverness, had three Irish visitors. We are told that when he refused to let them in, their leader made a

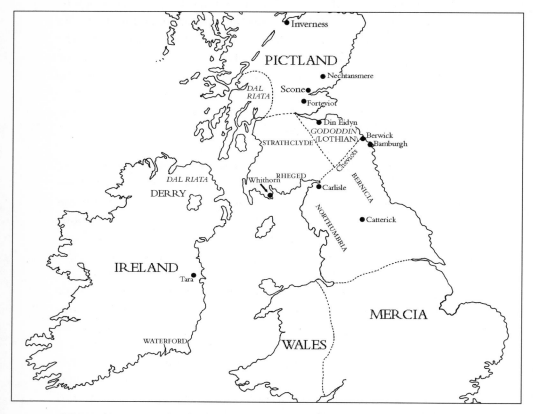

16 North Britain and Ireland, sixth century AD, with places mentioned in chapter 9

sign of the cross, and the heavily barred wooden doors flew open. This is one of many miracles attributed to Columba (521–97), a man of princely birth who had taken religious vows. There is a nice story that when he was sent to St Etchen to be made bishop, the saint ordained him presbyter by mistake. Columba saw in this the will of God, and never sought higher office; neither did his successors as abbot of Iona, where in 563 he founded a monastery. He and 12 companions had landed there after he had left Ireland, it is said in remorse at having been responsible for the deaths of 3,000 men in a battle over his insistence on retaining a copy of a psalter which he had made without the owner's permission.

Legend states that St Columba was a scourge of the druids, and made many converts among the Picts. Certainly he was the founder of the Celtic Church in Scotland, paralleling that in Ireland, with its monastic framework enclosing the ancient orders of the Roman Catholic Church.

According to Columba's first biographer Adamnan (627/8–704), sixth abbot of Iona, when Conall, king of the Dál Riata in Argyll, died in 574, Columba reluctantly consecrated Aedán (d. 608) as his successor. Aedán appears to have been a warlord in a tradition that reflected the imperial military policy of Rome, which resurfaced in the development of a Scottish nation. He represented an aggressive society, whose aspirations were measured by the acquisition of land, tribute, booty, and slaves, and whose fame by heroic deeds in battle. The patterns of that society were changing too. Towards the end of the sixth century, Urien, king of Rheged, and Riderch, king of the Strathclyde Britons, jointly besieged the Angles at Bamburgh. Urien's death in battle was the beginning of the end of Rheged, and initiated further disaster for the northern kingdoms. In about 600, partly in retaliation, a Christian force rode out from Edinburgh comprising men of Gododdin, Britons from north Wales and from Ayrshire, and possibly also Picts. Their mission was to attack the heathen Angles at Catterick. The Welsh heroic poem known as the *Gododdin*, attributed to the contemporary poet Aneirin, tells of 300 of these warriors, of whom only four returned. By 640 the Angles had moved north to occupy the region as far as the Forth, and the Gododdin are heard of no more.

Subsequently the Angles crossed to the other side of the Forth and occupied part of southern Pictland, but in 685 they were conclusively defeated at the famous battle of Nechtansmere, and withdrew. They were beaten again in 698, but turned the tables on the Picts in 711. Thereafter there were some sort of amicable relations between the two. The Pictish centre of power now moved south, to Scone or nearby Forteviot, with a boundary maintained between the two peoples. This became the southern border of a unified Scotland north of the Forth, when in 741 Oengus mac Fergus (c.690–761), who had become king of all the Picts in 729, and had distant family connections to the Dál Riata, subdued the various kings and warlords of the Irish Scots. This was effectively the first step along the way to a Scottish nation.

The ultimate cultural mix was further extended by Vikings from Norway and subsequently Denmark, who devastated Iona three times between 795 and 806, on the third occasion massacring 68 monks. Originally they came as predatory raiders, killing and looting along the coasts and through the northern and western islands, then also as settlers, who forcibly colonised huge tracts of land in the north and in the west as far as Argyll. In 839, in the course of a series of Viking campaigns of violence that lasted for many years, the Pictish king, his brother, their ruling elite, a king of Dál Riata, and a host of warriors lost their lives. Out of the ensuing political maelstrom, Cinead mac Ailpín, Kenneth mac Alpin (d. 858), a king of the Dál Riata who could claim descent also from Pictish royalty, emerged as king of both the Picts and the Dál Riata. By the beginning of the tenth century, his former subjects would now all regard themselves as 'Scots', occupying a united territory which was known as Alba, the former name for the whole of Britain. A hundred years later, and Gaelic, encouraged by the spread of Christianity from Iona, was the first language of Scotland except for the far north and south-east. Even more significantly, with the exception of the years 858–63, when his brother was king after his death, the dynasty of Kenneth I ruled Scotland until the Middle Ages, and the present royal family has claims to be his descendants.

Hadrian's Wall, the last frontier between Romans and non-Romans in the north, spanned the shortest distance between the west and east coasts of Britain except for the isthmus fortified by Agricola and Antoninus. The border between England and Scotland effectively begins at the western extremity of the wall, a few miles north of Carlisle, then follows the natural barrier of the Cheviots north-west to Berwick-on-Tweed, which changed hands several times in the Middle Ages. The wall, if only as a symbol of conquest of the island of Britain to the south of it, may have proved also to become a psychological boundary between two societies.

With the exception of the Orkneys and Shetland, which remained in Scandinavian hands until 1474, modern Scotland effectively came into being in 1018, when the Gaelic-speaking Malcolm II (*c*.945–1034) took Lothian and Strathclyde into his kingdom of Scotia. The language known as Scots developed from the form of English spoken by the Angles in south-east Scotland, to which elements accrued from the speech of the Scandinavians who, in the ninth century, drove a wedge between the Angles of Lothian and their countrymen to the south. In medieval Scotland Latin was the linguistic bridge between the speakers of Gaelic and Scots. Roman-British Christianity, however, made a far greater impact on Scotland than the Romans themselves, though at the time of the union of the Scottish and English parliaments in 1707 pro-unionists argued that an injection of English culture would be of similar benefit to Scotland as had been the Roman invasions of Britannia.

Empire is not a fashionable term today, and the beneficial contributions of the Romans and British to the peoples whom they conquered or whose territories they annexed in its name tend to be submerged beneath less honourable motives and actions. What benefits the Romans brought to Britannia were largely dissipated during the angry, confused years that followed their withdrawal. Scotland remained almost entirely untouched by Roman rule. Yet its contribution to peaceful development in parts of the former British empire has been out of all proportion to her population, and the influence of Scottish administrators, doctors, farmers, engineers, explorers, businessmen, manufacturers, educators, and religious leaders has often outweighed their numbers.

TIMELINES

BRITAIN		CLASSICAL WORLD	
BC			
c.8000–4000	Middle Stone Age in Scotland		
c.7600	Earliest known settlement in Scotland		
c.4000–2000	New Stone Age in Scotland		
c.3600–2450	Occupation of Skara Brae		
c.2800	Callanish Stones, Lewis		
c.2000–700	Bronze Age in Scotland	c.1200	Trojan War
c.1900–1400	Building of Stonehenge		
c.1000	First Celts in Scotland	753	Traditional date of founding of Rome
	Hill-forts, roundhouses	510–27	Era of Republican Rome
c.700–AD 500	Iron Age in Scotland	c.490–323	Golden age of Greece
c.700	Fortified settlements	442–438	Parthenon frieze (Elgin Marbles)
c.500	Crannogs	c.400	Celtic tribes invade Italy
c.200	Wheel-houses, souterrains	353–323	Conquests of Alexander the Great
c.200–AD 150	Broch building	264–146	Punic Wars: Rome v Carthage
c.150	Settlement of Celtic tribes in	108–100	Marius reorganises Roman army
	Scotland	58–49	Caesar is governor in Gaul
55 and 54	Caesar's invasions of Britain	44	Assassination of Caesar
AD			
		14	Death of Augustus
43	Claudius invades Britain	41	Death of Caligula
60	Revolt of Boudica	69–79	Vespasian is emperor
73	Petillius Cerialis in Scotland		
78	Agricola arrives in Britain		
79	Agricola invades Scotland	79	Eruption of Vesuvius
80	Agricola campaigns as far as the Tay	80	Opening of Colosseum
81	Clyde–Forth line fortified	81–96	Domitian is emperor
82	Agricola in Galloway		
83	Agricola campaigns beyond the		
	Forth		
84	Battle of Mons Graupius. End of	85–89	Wars in Dacia and Germany
	Agricola's terms of office		
86/7	Roman withdrawal to the Cheviots		
	Destruction of Inchtuthil		
c.105	Further withdrawal, to Solway–Tyne	98–117	Trajan is emperor
	line	113	Construction of Trajan's column
118	Disturbances in the north	117–138	Hadrian is emperor
122	Hadrian in Britain. Work begins on	117	Roman Empire at greatest level
	Hadrian's Wall	135	Destruction of Jerusalem
c.140	Lollius Urbicus invades Scotland	138–161	Antoninus is emperor
142–150	Building of Antonine Wall		
154–158	Trouble between the walls	161–180	Marcus Aurelius is emperor
c.169	Antonine Wall abandoned	162–166	Parthian wars
	Emergence of Maeatae	165–167	Plague spreads through Roman empire
178–184	Ulpius Marcellus governer in Britain	180–192	Commodus is emperor
c.180	Hadrian's Wall again the frontier		
c.185	Outposts in Scotland abandoned		
193–197	Clodius Albinus emperor in Britain	193–211	Septimius Severus is emperor
c.197	Virius Lupus appeases Caledonians and	197	Severus increases army pay and lifts
	Maeatae		ban on soldiers marrying
209	Severus invades Scotland	203	Arch of Severus

210	Caledonians and Maeatae make further trouble	212	Caracalla confers citizenship, and the privilege of paying taxes, on all free inhabitants of the empire
211	Caracalla abandons northern campaign	217	Assassination of Caracalla Completion of baths of Caracalla
c.215	Outpost forts in southern Scotland rebuilt. Establishment of *exploratores*	253–268	Gallienus is emperor
260–271	Dominion of Gaul (including Britannia)	270–275	Aurelian is emperor
286–296	Rule of Carausius (Allectus from 293)	285	Diocletian (emperor 284–305) divides empire into east and west
c.297	Constantius restores order and repairs Hadrian's Wall	292	Constantinius given charge of Britain, Gaul, and Spain
297	First mention of Picts	305–306	Constantinius emperor in west
306	Campaign against northern tribes	306–337	Rule of Constantine the Great
c.343	Destruction of outpost forts in southern Scotland. *Arcani* replace *exploratores*		Christianity becomes official religion of the Roman empire
353–364	Unrest in Britannia. Scots join Picts in raids around and across Hadrian's Wall	361–363	Rule of Julian the 'Apostate'
		364–375	Valentinian I emperor in west, Valens in east (364–378)
367	Picts, Scots and Attacotti joined by Franks and Saxons in plundering Britannia		
368	Theodosius restores order and repairs Hadrian's Wall. Outpost forts finally abandoned	c.375	Massive folk movement into central Europe from east begins
		379–395	Rule of Theodosius I. After him the division of the empire was permanent
382	Picts and Scots defeated by Magnus Maximus	391/2	Edicts of Theodosius I banning pagan worship
c.396–400	Stilicho campaigns against Picts and Scots	401	Alaric the Visigoth invades Italy
c.400–425	Irish raids against the coasts of Britain	404	Western empire ruled from Ravenna
410	'Rescript' of Honorius, that he could give no help to the province against outside attacks	406	Alans, Suevi, and Vandals occupy northern Gaul
		410	Alaric sacks Rome
c.425–450	St Ninian at Whithorn	c.415	Suevi and Vandals occupy Spain
429	Picts defeated in Britannia by St Germanus	418	Visigoths establish kingdoms at Toulouse and in Africa
c.430	Vortigern introduces Saxon mercenaries to oppose Picts	451	Aetius defeats Attila the Hun
446	Britons appeal to Aetius for help against Saxons	452	Pope Leo I (440–461) saves Rome by mediating with Attila
		455	Vandals sack Rome from the sea
c.450	Dál Riata begin to settle in Argyll	476	End of Roman empire in the west
559	Picts defeat Dál Riata	527–565	Rule of Justinian in the east. Justinian code of Roman law and golden age of Byzantine architecture
c.560	Southern Scotland comprises Gododdin, Strathclyde, and Rheged		
563–597	St Columba in Iona	597	Pope Gregory (590–604) sends (St) Augustine (d. 630) to convert the Anglo-Saxons
c.600	Gododdin defeat at Catterick; territory taken over by Angles		
741	Oengus mac Fergus, king of all the Picts, subdues Dál Riata	622	Traditional date for founding of Islam
		760	Foundation of Turkish empire
c.790	Beginning of Viking raids	800	Charlemagne (742–814) crowned in Rome as emperor of the west
843–858	Kenneth mac Alpin, king of Dál Riata and Picts	907	End of T'ang dynasty in China
1018	Malcolm II takes Lothian and Strathclyde into kingdom of Scotia	1053	Split between Church of Rome and the Church in the east
		1453	End of eastern Roman empire

PLACES TO VISIT – A SELECTION

Anthropological Museum, Marishal College, Aberdeen (01224 274 301): Pictish stones.

Bute Museum, Rothesay (01700 505 067): early crosses.

Callendar House, Falkirk (01324 503 770): display relating to Antonine Wall.

Dumfries Museum and Camera Obscura (01387 253 374): early Christian carved stones.

Dunrobin Castle Museum, Golspie, Sutherland (01408 633 177): Pictish carved stones, including ogham.

Elgin Museum (01343 543 675): early Christian carved stones.

Glasgow Museum and Art Gallery (0141 287 2000): reopening March 2006.

Groam House Museum, Rosemarkie, Invernessshire (01381 620 961): Pictish carved stones.

Hadrian's Wall: Centres include *Housesteads Roman Fort and Museum* (01434 344 363), *Roman Army Museum,* Carvoran (016977 47485), *Vindolanda Site and Chesterholm Museum* (01434 344 060).

Hunterian Museum, University of Glasgow (0141 330 4221): permanent displays of the Romans in Scotland – Army on campaign, Life on the frontier, Retreat, Religion, Antonine Wall (including distance-slabs). Also fine collection of Roman coins.

Huntly House Museum, Edinburgh (0131 529 4143): includes Roman exhibits from the vicinity.

Inverness Museum and Art Gallery (01463 237 114): Pictish carved stones.

Iona Abbey (01681 700 404): wide-ranging display of Christian carved stones.

Kilmartin House, Argyll (01546 510 278): regional centre and museum of history of culture, incorporating Celtic material.

Kinneil Museum, Kinneil Estate, Bo'ness (01506 778 530), a short walk from a fortlet site on the Antonine Wall: exhibition – Rome's northern frontier.

Meigle Museum, Perth and Kinrossshire (01828 640 612): outstanding collection of Pictish carved stones.

Museum of Antiquities, Newcastle upon Tyne (0191 222 7846/7849): incorporates Reticulum Project for schoolchildren featuring life in northern England during Roman times, Roman arms and armour, and a full-scale reconstruction of the temple of Mithras from Carrawburgh. The museum also houses the Hadrian's Wall Photographic Archive.

Museum nan Eilean, Stornoway (01851 709 266): exhibits illustrating the archaeology of Lewis and the town of Stornoway.

Museum of Scotland, Chambers Street, Edinburgh (0131 225 7534): significant Celtic and Roman material, including Bronze Age hoards and the Traprain Law treasure. Galleries cover Beginnings, Early People, and The Kingdom of the Scots.

Perth Museum and Art Gallery (01738 632 488): local history displays arranged thematically include sculpted stones.

Pictavia Visitor Centre, By Brechin Castle Centre, Haughmuir (01356 626241): Pictish life and culture, including symbol stones and the battle of Dunnichen (Nechtansmere).

St Andrews Cathedral Museum (01334 412 563): includes early Christian carved stones.

St Vigeans Museum, Arbroath (01786 450 000): Pictish carved stones. April to September.

Scottish Crannog Centre, Kenmore, Loch Tay (01887 830 583): reconstruction and displays, events and activities. Open March to November.

Shetland Museum, Lerwick (01595 880 432): includes material from Neolithic, Bronze Age, and Iron Age Shetland.

Tankerness House Museum, Kirkwall, Orkney (01856 873 191): includes material from Brough of Birsay, Buckquoy, and Gurness, and Pictish stones.

Tarbat Discovery Centre, Portmahomack, Ross-shire (01862 871 351): archaeology, including sculptured stones, of an eighth-century Pictish community.

Trimontium Romano-Celtic Exhibition, Melrose (01896 822 651): displays, activities, and events.

Tullie House Museum and Art Gallery, Carlisle (01228 534 781): material relating to Carlisle's two Roman forts and to the western part of Hadrian's Wall, and to life in Roman Carlisle.

Whithorn Priory and Museum, Dumfries and Galloway (01988 500 700). The museum has a good collection of early Christian sculptured stones. The archaeological excavations can be seen by visitors. Open April to October.

ARCHAEOLOGICAL SITES AND MONUMENTS (WITH MAP REFERENCES)

Neolithic
Balfarg and *Balbirnie*, Glenrothes, Fife: archaeological trail covering henge (NO 281 031) and stone circle (NO 285 029).
Ballochmyle (private ownership), East Ayrshire (NS 511 255): rock-face carvings.
Balnuaran of Clava, Invernessshire (NH 752 439): chambered cairns and standing stones.
Barnhouse, Orkney (HY 308 126): settlement.
Cairnholy, Dumfries and Galloway (NX 518 540): chambered tombs.
Cairnpapple, West Lothian (NS 987 717): ceremonial site.
Callanish, Lewis (NB 213 330): standing stones.
Camster, Caithness (ND 260 441): round cairns.
Capo, Aberdeenshire (NO 633 664): earthen barrow.
Croft Moraig (private ownership), Perthshire and Kinross (NN 797 472): stone circle.
Hill o' Many Stanes, Lybster, Caithness (ND 295 384): stone monuments.
Isbister, South Ronaldsay, Orkney (HY 470 845): chambered tomb.
Jarlshof, Shetland (HU 398 095): settlement.
Knap of Howar, Papa Westray, Orkney (HY 483 518): homestead.
Loanhead of Daviot, Aberdeenshire (NJ 747 288): stone circle with recumbent stone, and burial enclosure.
Lundin Links, Fife (NO 404 027): standing stones.
Machrie Moor, Arran (NR 900 325 to 912 323): stone circles and chambered tombs, also Bronze Age cairns and hut-circles.
Maes Howe, Orkney (HY 318 127): chambered tomb.
Ring of Brodgar, Orkney (HY 294 134): standing stones.
Skara Brae, Orkney (HY 231 188): settlement.
Stanydale, Shetland (HU 285 502): landscape and building.
Stenness, Orkney (HY 306 125): standing stones.
Temple Wood (NR 826 978), stone circle, and *Nether Largie South* (NR 828 979), chambered cairn, Argyll: elements of a landscape of monuments.

Brochs
Carn Liath, Brora, Sutherland (NC 870 013).
Clickhimin, Shetland (HU 464 408).
Dun Dornaigil, Sutherland (NC 457 450).
Dun Telve (NG 829 172) and *Dun Troddan* (NG 833 172), Glenelg, Ross and Cromarty.
Gurness, Orkney (HY 381 268): broch village, also Pictish house.
Midhowe, Rousay, Orkney (HY 371 305): also chambered tomb.

Mousa (Island of), Shetland (HU 457 237).
Nybster, Caithness (ND 370 361).
Torwoodlee, Galashiels (NT 465 384).

Hill-forts and settlements
The Brown Caterthun (NO 555 668) and *The White Caterthun* (NO 547 660): hill-fort settlements.
Burnswark Hill, Dumfries and Galloway (NY 186 787): hill-fort and Roman siege-works.
Castlelaw, Midlothian (NYT 229 638): hill-fort and souterrain.
The Chesters, Drem, East Lothian (NT 506 782): fortified settlement.
Dumyat, Bridge of Allan, Stirlingshire (NS 832 973): fort.
Edin's Hall, Preston, Berwickshire (NT 772 603): hill-fort enclosing broch.
Eildon Hill North (private ownership), Melrose (NT 555 328): hill-fort settlement, and Roman signal station.
Holyrood Park, Edinburgh (NT 27 73): forts.
Hownam Law, Kirk Yetholm, Roxburghshire (NT 796 220): hill-fort settlement.
Queen's View, Loch Tummel, Perthshire and Kinross (NN 863 601): roundhouse homestead.
Rispain Camp, Dumfries and Galloway (NX 429 399): rectangular fort.
Traprain Law, East Lothian (NT 580 746): hill-fort settlement.
Woden Law, Roxburghshire (NT 768 125): hill-fort. Nearby at Pennymuir (NT 755 140) are outlines of two
    Roman marching camps.

Souterrains
Ardestie (NO 502 344) and *Carlungie* (NO 511 359), Angus.
Crichton (private ownership), Midlothian (NT 400 619).
Culsh, Aberdeenshire (NJ 504 054).
Grain, Orkney (HY 441 116).
Pitcur (private ownership), Perthshire and Kinross (NO 253 374).
Rennibister, Orkney (HY 397 127).
Tealing, Angus (NO 412 381).

Roman forts and fortifications
Antonine Wall. Key sites, from west to east: Bearsden (NS 546 720), fort and bathhouse; Bar Hill (NS 708
    758), rampart, ditch, and fort wall; Croy Hill (NS 725 762), rampart and ditch; Seabegs Wood (NS 812
    792), rampart, ditch, and traces of military road; Rough Castle (NS 843 798), rampart, ditch, fort outline,
    and *lilia*; Watling Lodge (NS 863 798), well-preserved section of ditch; Callendar Park (NS 886 798),
    ditch; Kinneil (NS 977 803), fortlet outline with buildings marked.
Ardoch, Braco, Perthshire and Kinross (NN 840 100): well-preserved fort earthworks.
Birrens, Dumfries and Galloway (NY 218 752): remains of fort rampart and defensive ditches.
Castle Greg, West Calder (NT 050 592): fortlet rampart and double ditch.
Cramond, Edinburgh (NT 189 769): outlines of buildings. Due to be developed as a
    visitor centre.
Dere Street, Soutra, Midlothian (NT 450 580): section of Roman road.
Durisdeer, Dumfries and Galloway (NS 902 048): well-preserved fortlet defences.
Gask Ridge, Perthshire and Kinross. The best-preserved earthworks of the watch-
    towers are at Ardunie (NN 946 187) and Muir o' Fauld (NN 981 189).

Pictish
Aberlemno, Angus (NO 522 559): three symbol stones.
Burghead, Moray (NJ 109 691): fort remains (private ownership) and well. Probable site of Pictish naval base.
    The walls carried a frieze of carved bulls, of which two are in Burghead Library, and two in Elgin
    Museum.
Dunfallandy, Pitlochry (NN 946 565): symbol stone.
Sueno's Stone, Forres, Moray (NI 046 595): carved monument.
Yarrow, Selkirk (NT 348 274): sixth-century Christian inscribed stone.

SOURCES

CLASSICAL AUTHORS

★Aelius Spartianus and ★Julius Capitolinus
  Spartianus wrote between AD 293 and 305 biographies of Hadrian, Severus, Niger, Caracalla, and
  Geta; among the biographies written by Capitolinus in about AD 300 are Antoninus Pius and
  Marcus Aurelius.
  The Scriptores Historiae Augustae (Historia Augusta), volume I, tr. David Magie 1922, Heinemann (Loeb
  Classical Library), London, and Putnam's, New York
★Ammianus Marcellinus (c.AD 330–c.395)
  Born in Syrian Antioch. Served on the staff of Ursicinus, commander-in-chief of the army in the
  east. Subsequently prepared for the writing of his history of Rome, a continuation of Tacitus; in
  about 390 he wrote in Latin, his second language, 31 books, of which 17 survive.
  Res Gestae, tr. John C. Rolfe (3 vols) 1935–40, Harvard University Press (Loeb Classical Library),
  Cambridge, Mass., and Heinemann, London. Volume 3 includes *Excerpta Valesiana*, tr. John C. Rolfe
  1939.
★Caesar (Gaius Julius Caesar, 100–44 BC)
  Born in Rome. Governor of Gaul 58–49. Dictator of the Roman republic 49–44. Assassinated 44.
  Wrote in 51 seven books of his account of his wars in Gaul and Britain – the eighth is by Aulus
  Hirtius.
  The Gallic War, tr. H.J. Edwards 1917, Harvard University Press (Loeb Classical Library), Cambridge,
  Mass.
Cassius Dio (Cassius Dio Cocceianus, c.AD 160–c.235)
  Probably born in Bithynia. Served as consul (c.222) and then as governor of the province of Africa,
  and was consul again in 229. During the years 200–22, he prepared and wrote in Greek 80 books of
  his history of Rome from the landing of Aeneas to the death of Severus, of which 26 survive.
  Roman History, tr. Earnest Cary (9 vols) 1914–27, Harvard University Press (Loeb Classical Library),
  Cambridge, Mass.
★Claudian (Claudius Claudianus, c.AD 370–c.404)
  Born probably in Alexandria, and wrote in Greek until 395. His composition of
  public poems in Latin hexameters earned him a bronze statue in the Forum of Trajan.
  Claudian, tr. Maurice Platnauer (2 vols) 1976, Harvard University Press (Loeb Classical Library),
  Cambridge, Mass., and Heinemann, London
Herodian (Herodianus, c.AD 175–c.250)
  Born probably in Syrian Antioch. Wrote in Greek a history of Rome from the death of Marcus
  Aurelius to the accession of Gordian III in 238.
  History, tr. C.R. Whittaker (2 vols) 1969–70, Heinemann (Loeb Classical Library), London, and
  Harvard University Press, Cambridge, Mass.
Pliny the Elder (Gaius Plinius Secundus, AD 23–79)
  Born at Comum (Lake Como) of a well-to-do family. Governor in Africa, Gaul, and Spain. Wrote
  numerous works, including the 37 books of his scientific treatise, *Naturalis Historia*.
  Natural History, volume II, Books 3–7, tr. H. Rackham 1942, Heinemann, London, and Harvard
  University Press (Loeb Classical Library), Cambridge, Mass.
★Statius (Publius Papinius Statius, c.AD 45–96)
  Born in Naples, and, like his father, won prizes for poetry at festivals. He spent 12 years writing an
  epic poem, *Thebaid*; *Silvae* is a collection of occasional and miscellaneous pieces.

Silvae, ed. and tr. D.R. Shackleton Bailey 2003, Harvard University Press (Loeb Classical Library), Cambridge, Mass., and London
★Suetonius (Gaius Suetonius Tranquillus, *c.*AD 70–*c.*140)
Born of an equestrian family who probably came from Algiers. He was director of the imperial libraries and then chief of Hadrian's personal secretariat, which gave him access to court archives. His series of biographies of the Caesars is the only one of his numerous historical works to survive.
The Twelve Caesars, tr. Robert Graves, rev. and introd. Michael Grant 1979, Penguin Books, Harmondsworth
★Tacitus (Publius (or Gaius) Cornelius Tacitus, AD 56/7–*c.*117)
Born in northern Italy or southern Gaul, of an equestrian family, and studied public speaking in Rome. He had a steady rise in politics, and was suffect consul in 97. His biography of his father-in-law, of which there is a critical assessment above in chapter 4, is the only source of information on the crucial campaigns of Agricola in north Britain. His major works are known as the *Annals* (published 115–17) and the *Histories* (published 105–8), describing the history of Rome from AD 14 to 96; the surviving books cover the years 14–37, 47–66, and, in greater detail, 69–70.
The Agricola and the Germania, tr. H. Mattingly, rev. S.A. Handford 1970, Penguin Books, Harmondsworth
The Annals of Imperial Rome, tr. Michael Grant 1989 (rev. edn), Penguin Books, London
The Histories, tr. Kenneth Wellesley 1962, Penguin Books, Harmondsworth
De Vita Agricolae, ed. R.M. Ogilvy and Sir Ian Richmond 1967, Oxford University Press, Oxford
★New translations in *The Last Frontier*

MODERN AUTHORS

Armit, Ian 1997, *Celtic Scotland*, Batsford, London
Armit, Ian 1998, *Scotland's Hidden History*, Tempus, Stroud and Charleston
Auguet, Roland 1994 (new edn), *Cruelty and Civilization: The Roman Games*, Routledge, London and New York
Bailey, Geoff B., with reconstructions by Michael Moore 2003, *The Antonine Wall: Rome's Northern Frontier*, Falkirk Council
Bede, tr. Leo Sherley-Price, rev. R.E. Latham 1968 (rev. edn), *A History of the English Church and People*, Penguin Books, Harmondsworth and New York
Benario, Herbert W. 2000, *Hadrian*, De Imperatoribus Romanis: An Online Encyclopaedia of Roman Emperors
Birley, Anthony 1964, *Life in Roman Britain*, Batsford, London, and Putnam's, New York
Birley, Anthony R. 1988 (rev. edn), *Septimius Severus: The African Emperor*, Routledge, London and New York
Birley, Anthony 2002, *Garrison Life at Vindolanda: A Band of Brothers*, Tempus, Stroud and Charleston
Birley, Robin 1991, *Garrison Life on the Roman Frontier*, Roman Army Museum Publications, Greenhead
Bowman, Alan K. 1994, *Life and Letters on the Roman Frontier: Vindolanda and Its People*, British Museum Press, London
Breeze, David J. 1982, *The Northern Frontiers of Roman Britain*, Batsford, London
Breeze, David J. 1996, *Roman Scotland*, Batsford, London
Burleigh, J.H.S. 1960, *A Church History of Scotland*, Oxford University Press, London, New York, and Toronto
Burn, Andrew Robert 1953, *Agricola and Roman Britain*, English Universities Press, London
Carcopino, Jérôme, ed. Henry T. Rowell, tr. E.O. Lorimer 1956, *Daily Life in Ancient Rome: The People and the City at the Height of the Empire*, Penguin Books, Harmondsworth
Cary, M. 1957 (2nd edn), *A History of Rome: Down to the Reign of Constantine*, Macmillan, London and New York
Chadwick, Nora 1970, *The Celts*, Penguin Books, Harmondsworth and New York
Clarke, John 1950, 'Excavations at Milton (Tassiesholm) in Season 1950', *Transactions of the Dumfriesshire and Galloway Natural History and Antiquarian Society*, 3rd series, volume xxviii, pp. 199ff

Close-Brooks, Joanna and Stevenson, Robert B.K. 1982, *Dark Age Sculpture: A Selection from the Collections of the National Museum of Antiquities of Scotland*, National Museum of Antiquities of Scotland and HMSO, Edinburgh

Collis, Peter 2003, *The Celts: Origins, Myths & Inventions*, Tempus, Stroud

Connolly, Peter 1988, *Tiberius Claudius Maximus: The Cavalryman*, Oxford University Press, Oxford

Connolly, Peter 1988, *Tiberius Claudius Maximus: The Legionary*, Oxford University Press, Oxford

Connolly, Peter 1998, *The Ancient City: Life in Classical Athens & Rome*, Oxford University Press, Oxford

de Jersey, Philip 1996, *Celtic Coinage in Britain*, Shire Publications, Princes Risborough

de la Bédoyère, Guy 2001, *Eagles over Britannia*, Tempus, Stroud and Charleston

Dickson, Camilla and Dickson, James H. 2000, *Plants & People in Ancient Scotland*, Tempus, Stroud and Charleston

Divine, David 1969, *The North-West Frontier: A Military Study of Hadrian's Wall*, Macdonald, London

Donaldson, Gordon 1974, *Scotland: The Shaping of a Nation*, David & Charles, Newton Abbott and North Pomfret

Driscoll, Stephen 2002, *Alba: The Gaelic Kingdom of Scotland AD 800–1124*, Birlinn, Edinburgh

Duncan, A.A.M. (reprint with revisions) 1978, *Scotland: The Making of the Kingdom*, Oliver and Boyd, Edinburgh

Edwards, Kevin J. and Ralston, Ian B.M. (eds) 2003 (new edn), *Scotland after the Ice Age: Environment, Archaeology and History, 8000 BC–AD 1000*, Edinburgh University Press, Edinburgh

Ellis, Peter Berresford 1994 (new edn), *Caesar's Invasion of Britain*, Constable, London

Ellis, Peter Berresford 1995, *Celtic Women: Women in Celtic Society and Literature*, Constable, London

Foster, Sally M. 1996, *Picts, Gaels and Scots*, Batsford, London

French, Roger and Greenaway, Frank (eds) 1986, *Science in the Early Roman Empire: Pliny the Elder, His Sources and Influence*, Croom Helm, London and Sydney

Frere, Sheppard 1978 (rev. edn), *Britannia: A History of Roman Britain*, Routledge & Kegan Paul, London and Boston

Grant, Michael 1996 (2nd, rev. edn), *The Fall of the Roman Empire*, Weidenfeld & Nicolson, London

Green, Kevin 1986, *The Archaeology of the Roman Economy*, Batsford, London

Green, Miranda 1995, *Celtic Goddesses: Warriors, Virgins and Mothers*, British Museum Press, London

Green, Miranda J. (ed.) 1996 (new edn), *The Celtic World*, Routledge, London and New York

Gregory, Richard A. 2001, 'Excavations by the late G.D.B. Jones and C.M. Daniels along the Moray Forth littoral', *Proceedings of the Society of Antiquaries of Scotland*, volume 131, pp. 177–222

Hackett, General Sir John (ed.) 1989, *Warfare in the Ancient World*, Sidgwick & Jackson, London

Hamey, L.A. and J.A. 1981, *The Roman Engineers*, Cambridge University Press, Cambridge

Hanson, W. S. 1987, *Agricola and the Conquest of the North*, Batsford, London

Henderson, Isabel 1967, *The Picts*, Thames and Hudson, London

Herman, Arthur 2001, *The Scottish Enlightenment: The Scots' Invention of the Modern World*, Fourth Estate, London

Hoffmann, Birgitta 2001, 'Archaeology versus Tacitus's Agricola, a First-Century Worst Case Scenario', lecture given to the Theoretical Archaeology group conference, Dublin, 15 December

Hunterian Museum 1992, *The Wealth of Nations: A Guide to the Permanent Exhibition Mounted in the Coin Gallery*, University of Glasgow

Kamm, Antony 1995, *The Romans: An Introduction*, Routledge, London and New York

Kamm, Antony 1999, *The Israelites: An Introduction*, Routledge, London and New York

Kamm, Antony 2002, *Julius Caesar: A Beginner's Guide*, Hodder & Stoughton, London

Kenworthy, James (ed.) 1981, *Agricola's Campaigns in Scotland*, Edinburgh University Press, Edinburgh

Keppie, Lawrence 1979, *Roman Distance Slabs from the Antonine Wall*, Hunterian Museum, University of Glasgow

Keppie, Lawrence 1984, *The Making of the Roman Army: From Republic to Empire*, Batsford, London

Keppie, Lawrence 1986, *Scotland's Roman Remains*, John Donald, Edinburgh

Laing, Lloyd and Jenny 1993, *The Picts and the Scots*, Alan Sutton, Stroud and Dover, NH

Lewis, Charlton T. and Short, Charles (eds) 1879, *A Latin Dictionary*, Oxford University Press, Oxford

Lynch, Michael 1992 (new edn), *Scotland: A New History*, Pimlico, London

The Mabinogion, tr. Gwyn Jones and Thomas Jones 1974, Dent, London, and Dutton, New York

Macinnes, Lesley 1984, 'Brochs and the Roman Occupation of Lowland Scotland', *Proceedings of the Society of Antiquaries of Scotland*, volume 114, pp. 235–49

Manley, John 2002, *AD 43 The Roman Invasion of Britain: A Reassessment*, Tempus, Stroud and Charleston

Markale, Jean, tr. A. Mygind, C. Hauch, and P. Henry 1986, *Women of the Celts*, Inner Traditions, Rochester (VT)

Mason, David J.P. 2003, *Roman Britain and the Roman Navy*, Tempus, Stroud and Charleston

Maxwell, Gordon S. 1989, *The Romans in Scotland*, Mercat Press, Edinburgh

Miller, S.N. (ed.) 1953, *The Roman Occupation of South-Western Scotland*, Robert Maclehose, University Press, Glasgow

Myers, J.N.L. 1986, *The English Settlements*, Oxford University Press, Oxford

National Monuments Record 2001, *Roman Britain: Historical Map and Guide*, Ordnance Survey, Southampton

Ordnance Survey 1989, *Hadrian's Wall: Historical Map and Guide*, Southampton

Peacock, Phoebe 2001, *Lucius Verus*, De Imperatoribus Romanis: An Online Encyclopaedia of Roman Emperors

Percival, John 1976, *The Roman Villa*, Batsford, London

Piggott, Stuart (ed.) 1962, *The Prehistoric Peoples of Scotland*, Routledge and Kegan Paul, London

Piggott, Stuart 1982, *Scotland before History*, Edinburgh University Press, Edinburgh

Piggott, Stuart 1985 (new edn), *The Druids*, Thames and Hudson, London

Pollard, Tony and Morrison, Alex 1996, *The Early Prehistory of Scotland*, Edinburgh University Press, Edinburgh

Pomeroy, Sarah B. 1994, *Goddesses, Whores, Wives and Slaves: Women in Classical Antiquity*, Pimlico, London

Powell, T. G. E. 1958, *The Celts*, Thames and Hudson, London

Renfrew, Jane 1985, *Food and Cooking in Roman Britain: History and Recipes*, English Heritage

Ritchie, Anna 1977, *The Kingdom of the Picts*, Chambers, Edinburgh

Ritchie, Anna 1989, *Picts: An Introduction to the Life of the Picts and the Carved Stones in the Care of the Secretary of State for Scotland*, HMSO, Edinburgh

Ritchie, Anna and Breeze, David J. 1991, *Invaders of Scotland: An Introduction to the Archaeology of the Romans, Scots, Angles and Vikings, Highlighting the Monuments in the Care of the Secretary of State for Scotland*, HMSO, Edinburgh

Ritchie, Anna and Graham 1998, *Scotland: An Oxford Archaeological Guide*, Oxford University Press, Oxford and New York

Ritchie, Graham and Anna 1985 (new edn), *Scotland: Archaeology and Early History*, Thames and Hudson, London

Robertson, Anne S., rev. and ed. Lawrence Keppie 2001 (5th edn), *The Antonine Wall: A Handbook to the Surviving Remains*, Glasgow Archaeological Society, Glasgow

Royle, Trevor (new edn) 1993, *The Mainstream Companion to Scottish Literature*, Mainstream Publishing, Edinburgh and London

Salway, Peter 1981, *Roman Britain*, Oxford University Press, Oxford and New York

Salway, Peter 1993, *The Oxford Illustrated History of Roman Britain*, Oxford University Press, Oxford and New York

Sandys, Sir John Edwin (ed.) 1913 (2nd edn), *A Companion to Latin Studies*, Cambridge University Press, Cambridge

Senior, Alan 2003, *The Romans in Moray – and Beyond*, Moray Council website

Shelton, Jo-Ann 1988, *As the Romans Did: A Sourcebook in Roman Social History*, Oxford University Press, Oxford and New York

Shirley, Elizabeth 2001, *Building a Roman Legionary Fortress*, Tempus, Stroud and Charleston

Skene, William F. 1886 (2nd edn), *Celtic Scotland* (3 volumes), David Douglas, Edinburgh

Smith, Beverley Ballin and Banks, Iain (eds) 2002, *In the Shadow of the Brochs: The Iron Age in Scotland*, Tempus, Stroud and Charleston

Smyth, Alfred P. 1984, *Warlords and Holy Men: Scotland AD 80–1000*, Edward Arnold, London

Sorrell, Alan, ed. Mark Sorrell, 1981, *Reconstructing the Past*, Batsford, London

Stobart, J.C., rev. W.S. Maguinness and H.H. Scullard 1961 (4th edn), *The Grandeur That Was Rome*, Sidgwick and Jackson, London

Sutherland, Elizabeth 1994, *In Search of the Picts: A Celtic Dark Age Nation*, Constable, London

Thomas, Charles 2003 (new edn), *Christian Celts: Messages and Images*, Tempus, Stroud and Charleston

Todd, Malcolm 2004, 'Julius Agricola, Gnaeus (AD 40–93)', *Oxford Dictionary of National Biography*, Oxford University Press, Oxford

Vindolanda Tablets Online, http://vindolanda.csad.ox.ac.uk/

Vogt, Joseph, tr. Janet Sondheimer 1967, *The Decline of Rome: The Metamorphosis of Ancient Civilization*, Weidenfeld & Nicolson, London

Watson, William J. 1993 (new edn), *The History of the Celtic Place-Names of Scotland*, Birlinn, Edinburgh

Webster, Graham 1985 (3rd edn), *The Roman Imperial Army: Of the First and Second Centuries AD*, A. and C. Black, London

Webster, Graham 1993 (rev. edn), *The Roman Invasion of Britain*, Routledge, London and New York

Webster, Graham 1993 (rev. edn), *Boudica: The British Revolt against Rome AD 60*, Routledge, London and New York

Webster, Graham 2003 (reissue of rev. edn 1993), *Rome Against Caratacus: The Roman Campaigns in Britain AD 48–58*, Routledge, London and New York

Weigel, Richard D. 1998, *Antoninus Pius*, De Imperatoribus Romanis: An Online Encyclopaedia of Roman Emperors

Wells, Colin 1992 (2nd edn), *The Roman Empire*, Fontana Press, London

Wilson, Allan 2001, 'The Novantae and Romanization in Galloway', *Transactions of the Dumfriesshire and Galloway Natural History and Antiquarian Society*, 3rd Series, volume lxxv, pp. 73–131.

Woolliscroft, D.J. 2000, 'More Thoughts on Why the Romans Failed to Conquer Scotland', *Scottish Archaeological Journal*, volume 22. 2, pp. 111–22.

Woolliscroft, D.J. 2002, *The Roman Frontier on the Gask Ridge, Perth and Kinross: An Interim Report on the Roman Gask Project 1995–2000*, Archaeopress, Oxford

Woolliscroft, D.J. and Hoffmann, B. 2002, *The Roman Gask Project: Annual Report 2002* (Internet version)

Woolliscroft, D.J. and Hoffmann, B. 2003, *The Roman Gask Project: Annual Report 2003* (Internet version)

Wormald, Jenny 1991 (new edn), *Court, Kirk, and Community: Scotland 1470–1625*, Edinburgh University Press, Edinburgh

INDEX